JUDSON PRESS
PUBLISHERS SINCE 1824

To Serve This Present Age

Social Justice Ministries in the Black Church

Danielle L. Ayers and Reginald W. Williams Jr.

JUDSON PRESS
PUBLISHERS SINCE 1824

Join our mailing list for updates and special offers.
www.judsonpress.com/mailing_list.cfm

Unless otherwise noted, Scriptures are quoted from the New Revised Standard Version of the Bible, copyright © 1989 by the Division of Christian Education of the National Council of the Churches of Christ in the United States of America. Used by permission. All rights reserved.

Scriptures marked KJV are from the King James Version of the Bible.

Library of Congress Cataloging-in-Publication Data
Ayers, Danielle L.
    To serve this present age : social justice ministries in the Black church / Danielle L. Ayers and Reginald W. Williams Jr. — 1st ed.
        p. cm.
    ISBN 978-0-8170-1728-6 (pbk. : alk. paper) 1. African American churches. 2. African Americans—Religion. 3. Church work. 4. Social justice—Religious · aspects—Christianity. I. Williams, Jr. Reginald W. II. Title.
    BR563.N4A94 2013
    261.8089'96073—dc23
                                                                                2012034319

Printed in the U.S.A.
First Edition, 2013.

Contents

Foreword

Any serious student of the black religious experience in the black Atlantic (or the three Americas) will attest to the fact that there is not now—nor has there ever been—anything remotely resembling a monolithic black church.

The diversity of beliefs, the disparate—and at times dichotomous—approaches to addressing (or ignoring) the various social milieus in which the churches sat or sit, and the distinct differences between the understandings of what it meant or means to be a black "Christian" or (Muslim) in Brazil, as opposed to Birmingham; in Virginia as opposed to the Virgin Islands; in Colombia, South America, as opposed to Columbus, Georgia, or Columbus, Ohio—that diversity, that disparateness and those differences make the notion of a "monolithic black church" absurd.

Black Christian practitioners of Candomblé, vodun, and Santeria live in a different world than black Christian followers of T. D. Jakes, Creflo Dollar, and Noel Jones. The belief system of African-descended Christians who understand clearly that they live in a world where the oppressor controls their social reality and where their religious beliefs help them to fight that oppressor, neutralize that oppressor, or end that oppression is in a different world from the belief system of African Americans who do not understand "casino capitalism" as an ideology diametrically opposed to the teachings of the Carpenter from Capernaum.

There is a major difference between trying to get free (liberation) and trying to get rich (ostentation), yet both kinds of Christians are considered to be parts of the black church.

Some black Christians stay away from "politics" or social justice issues and ministry that address the harsh realities of black life in America, while other black Christians believe the church cannot be the church if it avoids the heart of prophetic ministry, which is social justice. Yet the diversity within the black church experience does not stop with that simple division of "this worldly/ other worldly." It gets much more complex.

Many black Christian social justice advocates who fight against racism, for instance, unequivocally embrace homophobia and heterosexism as foundational points in their theology. The same blacks who stood with Dr. Martin Luther King Jr. in his fight against racism and segregation walked away from Dr. Martin Luther King Jr. in his fight against militarism and "casino capitalism."

The diversity in the black church tradition has a long, complex history. Two centuries before Dr. Martin Luther King Jr., there were some black Christians who stood with Gabriel Prosser, Denmark Vesey, Nat Turner, and Harriet Tubman in their "by any means necessary" confrontational approach to liberation of the enslaved Africans. There were also, however, many more black Christians—including Harriet Tubman's husband!—who opposed Prosser, Vesey, Turner, and Tubman's methodologies. They saw cooperation, collaboration, and "gradualism" as the best methodologies for the liberation of the enslaved Africans.

Even within the same denominations widely different (and differing) theologies and interpretations of Scripture demonstrate the multilayered texture of the black religious experience and the highly diverse nature of the black church in the Americas. Bishop Henry McNeal Turner and Bishop Alexander Payne in the nineteenth-century African Methodist Episcopal Church are classic examples of two black clergypersons being at opposite ends of the pole in the same denomination. Dr. Martin Luther King Jr. and Dr. J. H. Jackson in the twentieth-century Baptist church are also classic examples of "east and west" in the same denomination when it came to addressing social justice issues.

For the student (or the reader) who is new to the highly complex nature of the black church, however, the issues of social justice and the church of Jesus Christ, which Rev. Reginald Williams and Min. Danielle Ayers address in this volume, will not only seem "novel," but will also be completely off the radar scope of what is understood to be in the purview of "religion" or the "spiritual."

One reason for this troubling anomaly has to do with the media and its skewed coverage of the black church in the Americas. Another of the many reasons for this disturbing fact has to do with the limited understanding of "this present age" when it comes to the black church's own history, own "story," and own rich legacy and heritage.

For at least half a century now (as of this writing), the media has portrayed a binary image, a "split-screen" presentation, of the black church in the United States. Dr. Martin Luther King Jr. is presented as representing one side of that picture, leading marches, having sit-ins, and advocating for social change and the dismantling of the racist structures of society in the United States.

Bishop T. D. Jakes is presented as representing the opposite side of that split-screen image. Where King led marches, Jakes holds mega-conferences. King ended segregated seating in public facilities. Jakes gets "bound" women loose and builds up men (macho, United States, Promise Keeper, superhero style). King addressed the social. Jakes addresses the personal. That is how the media portrays these two black clergymen.

The media has even officially labeled Bishop T. D. Jakes as "the next Billy Graham," and that labeling is telling, because where Dr. Martin Luther King Jr. confronted an evil government (to use R. Drew Smith's terminology),[1] Billy Graham cooperated with that government. Graham would not march with King (not even in the 1963 March on Washington), nor would he take a stand alongside King in opposition to many of the unjust policies of the U.S. government.

Graham, in fact, was the "pastor of the presidents." King has been portrayed as a prophet (like Amos) whose allegiance was to God, while Graham was portrayed as a priest (like Amaziah) whose allegiance was to government.

With that binary image portrayed on the screens of American imagery, King gets labeled as "controversial" and "confrontational" and as a "radical" and a leader of protests. Jakes (and Graham) are shown to be comforting, pastoral, and priestly. King is shown on one side of the screen as a "rebel" lumped together with Jesse Jackson and Al Sharpton (other rebels), while Jakes is shown on the other side of the screen as a "reverend" in the company of Creflo Dollar, Noel Jones, Billy Graham, and Joel Osteen.

Even more disturbing is how, according to its own definitions, the media moves King out of ministry into a category it labels "civil rights leader." King is portrayed as an agitator, and little to no mention is made of the fact that he was a pastor of a black church, trained theologically at Crozer Theological Seminary (earning a MDiv) and Boston University (earning a PhD in ethics), and preaching every Sunday in a pulpit before believers in the Lord, Jesus Christ. In fact, King's sermons mysteriously get labeled as "speeches" and "messages" by the media, and his role as a minister of the gospel is completely hidden from public view.

Jakes's men's conferences and 'Woman Thou Art Loosed' conferences, his megachurch in Dallas and his recordings which espouse the theology he embraces—a theology which is heard in songs from the "prosperity genre" such as "Bless Me (The Prayer of Jabez)" and "God Favored Me" (songs which are sung all over Black America) get lifted up by the media as the other image of the black church, and lost in that binary misrepresentation are the thousands of churches where social justice is just as much a part of who they are and what they do as shouting for Jesus is!

For millions of black Christians, the black church is not an "either/or" option. It is a "both/and" reality—both social justice *and* shouting for Jesus. It is that focus that these two authors, Williams and Ayers, bring to the attention of the reading public in this volume.

The authors use Charles Wesley's hymn "A Charge to Keep I Have" as their starting point for discussing the how-to's of doing social justice ministries. Their stated objective is "to serve this present age." That objective is both exciting and challenging for me. It is exciting because this present age is vastly different from my parents' age and my grandparents' age.

Putting the gospel of Jesus Christ "in a cup"[2] that this present age can recognize is a daunting task in and of itself. Making the gospel relevant to parishioners raised on Thomas Dorsey's, James Cleveland's, and Mahalia Jackson's music *and* parishioners raised on Common's, Salt-N-Pepa and Talib Kweli's music is difficult enough. Brandee Jasmine Mimitzraiem describes that exasperating experience in her essay "Too Young to Be Black."[3] Mimitzraiem makes a powerful point!

The painful part of what Dr. Mimitzraiem does *not* talk about when it comes to "this present age" is why I call Williams and Ayers's objective challenging. "This present age" of black believers has been brought up (for the most part) with no concept of the long, complex, and powerful history of the black church in the three Americas in general and the black church in North America in particular.

Serving "this present age" and making social justice ministry relevant for "this present age" does not mean starting with KRS-One or Jay Z. It means starting with the brush-arbor worship of Africans in the 1700s, examining the "invisible institution" of the black church in the 1800s, and comparing Gullah Jack and Boukman, the ring shout of the low country, and the spirit possession of Candomblé and vodun.

It means helping "this present age" connect the dots between the various (and varied) parts of their African religious heritage and the God of Moses and Miriam, the God of Jesus and Jarena Lee, the God of Isaiah and Ida B. Wells, the God of Matthew and Marley, and the God of Tertullian and Tupac.

Reginald Williams and Danielle Ayers have tackled an awesome objective in writing this book. It is an objective that is both exciting and challenging; and it is an objective that they invite all readers (and all of those who love the Lord) to embrace. Whether they succeed in reaching their objective will be determined by what *you* do after reading their compelling argument and excellent examples.

Rev. Dr. Jeremiah A. Wright Jr.
Pastor Emeritus
Trinity United Church of Christ
Chicago, Illinois

NOTES

1. See R. Drew Smith, *New Day Begun: African American Churches and Civic Culture in Post–Civil Rights America* (Durham, NC: Duke University Press, 2003) and *Long March Ahead: African American Churches and Public Policy in Post–Civil Rights America* (Durham, NC: Duke University Press, 2004).

2. "In a cup I can recognize" is a statement that comes from the ministry of Dr. John W. Kinney, dean of the Samuel DeWitt Proctor School of Theology at Virginia Union University and pastor of Ebenezer Baptist Church in Beaver Dam, Virginia. Dr. Kinney shares the autobiographical anecdote about what was said to him by an octogenarian on his first Sunday back in the pulpit after receiving his PhD from Columbia University and Union Theological Seminary in New York. He says he was "on fire" as he preached to ordinary country folk in Beaver Dam, Virginia, exhorting them concerning the importance of embracing the black experience in its totality and ridding themselves of the grave clothes of racism, segregation, and slave mentalities. At the end of the service as his members passed out of the sanctuary shaking his hand, congratulating him on his PhD, and trying to make "nice" comments about a sermon none of them understood, the octogenarian said to him as she put her hand on his solar plexus and pressed: "Son, you have a hot, bubbling, rich fountain burning right here; and it is a fountain from a well that is going to quench the thirst of thousands of people! I can feel it. It's right here!" I could hear it flowing and overflowing this morning as you preached, son. It is a rich fountain. I can tell it! But, if you want me to drink from your fountain, next time put it in a cup I can recognize!"

3. See Brandee Jasmine Mimitzraiem, "Too Young to Be Black: The Intergenerational Compatibility of Black Theology," in *Walk Together Children: Black and Womanist Theologies, Church and Theological Education,* ed. Dwight N. Hopkins and Linda E. Thomas (Eugene, OR: Cascade Books, 2009).

Acknowledgments

In 1963 Dr. Martin Luther King Jr. stood on the steps of the Lincoln Memorial and opened his famous "I Have a Dream" speech with these words: "Five score years ago, a great American, in whose symbolic shadow we stand today, signed the Emancipation Proclamation." In that same spirit, it has to be acknowledged that over the centuries both known and unknown individuals, in whose symbolic shadows humankind stands, labored in the vineyard of social justice against great odds. However, since the arrival of the first Africans in Jamestown, Virginia, the fight for freedom, justice, equality, and human rights has been rooted in the church. As early as the 1800s, clergy and lay leaders stood against oppressive structures. For example, the Reverend Nat Turner gave leadership to a slave revolt in Southampton County, Virginia, in hopes of breaking free from the institution of slavery. This is one example of how this rich tradition of engaging in social justice has been steeped in the black church. It is the obligation of the current generation to continue this legacy.

Many pastors and laypersons in the black church continue to uphold the charge to do justice, love mercy, and walk humbly before God in an age of prosperity and inspirational preaching. In 2008 and 2012 we witnessed the election and re-election of the United States's first President of African descent. Although this is a major step forward, the state of the nation's economy and political discourse and the persistence of various social issues continue to beckon faith communities, especially pastors and church leadership, to creatively care for bodies and souls. The state of public education (lack of funding, high dropout rates, excess of students academically unprepared for higher education, etc.) and high unemployment, especially in the African American community, are two examples that summon the church to the call of social justice.

It is with this heritage in mind that I thank God for keeping me until I answered the call. I want to lovingly acknowledge my parents, Anderson and Regenia Ayers, my brother Michael, my aunt Georgia who introduced me to the Lily of the Valley, and the rest of my family. I reverently acknowledge a wonderful set of mentors who have and continue to offer support, direction, and correction: Dr. Frederick D. Haynes III, Dr. Jeremiah A. Wright Jr., Dr. Iva E. Carruthers, Mrs. Edna Pemberton, and Rev. Rick Hill. I especially thank Dr. Haynes for allowing me to spread my wings. I appreciatively acknowledge the cherished circle of individuals whom I am privileged to call friends over many years. Your enduring prayers, trustworthiness, and cheerleading have kept me through it all. Lastly, I want to thank the staff and church family of Friendship-West Baptist Church in Dallas, Texas, for supporting the minister of justice.

Danielle Ayers

I truly believe in the communal concept of Ubuntu, which declares, "I am because we are, and because we are, therefore I am." I am grateful to God for God's faithfulness in spite of my feebleness. God is great and greatly to be praised. I am grateful to God for those in the village who have invested themselves in my humble efforts. I am grateful to the ancestors who have walked this way that we may walk this way. I especially honor my mother in this moment who has passed beyond the veil of time to new traffic in eternity. Your spirit never leaves me, and I carry you everywhere I go.

I am grateful for Rev. Dr. Jeremiah Wright Jr., who extended me an opportunity for six and a half years to serve as the associate pastor for justice ministries at Trinity United Church of Christ.

Your cultural integrity, selfless service, and commitment to God and the people of God have planted seeds around the world that are blossoming and blooming. Thank you for investing yourself in the soil of this soul. To Dr. Iva Carruthers, I am grateful for your model of commitment to the cause of the liberation of African people worldwide. Your strength is absolutely amazing, and I thank God for you. I am grateful for other mentors who have and continue to offer direction, assistance, support, and correction when needed: Rev. Dr. Yvonne Delk, Rev. Dr. Alison Gise Johnson, Mrs. Mary Crayton, Dr. John W. Kinney, Dr. Miles Jerome Jones, Bro. Kevin Tyson, Rev. Dr. Frederick Douglass Haynes III, Rev. Dr. D. Mitchell Ford, and Rev. Dr. Michael L. Pfleger.

I am grateful to the members of Trinity United Church of Christ who allowed me the privilege of serving as their Associate Pastor for Justice Ministries for six and a half years. I am pleased, proud, and privileged to now serve as the pastor of First Baptist Church of University Park. I am grateful for your warm spirit, willingness to work, and witness for our God as we seek to live the love of Christ.

Last but not least, I am grateful to God for my family. Dr. Reginald W. Williams Sr., I count it a great privilege to be named after you. Thank you for teaching me about Jesus and justice, the Almighty and African people! You are my hero, and I love you. To my brother, Rev. Matthew Williams, and sister, Joy Williams, thank you for your support and love. You don't choose family, but if I could have, I couldn't have chosen a more wonderful brother and sister. To my wife, Nikita, thank you for your support and love. You are a living lesson on what love looks like, and I'm grateful for the gift that is you! To my daughters, Nia and Laila, words cannot express how much I love you. This book is part of your daddy's efforts to try to see to it that you are left with a better world than the one your daddy entered. I pray my efforts will do just that!

This book is dedicated to the memory of my mother, Atty. Marcelle Hambrick Williams. Thank you for your love, which extends even beyond death. I feel you with me each step of the way!

Acknowledgments

Dr. Colleen Birchett, thank you for your patience and thorough, thoughtful reflection. You are a gem. Finally, to Rev. Rebecca Irwin-Diehl, Ms. Lisa Blair, and the staff at Judson Press, we thank you for your meaningful ministry!

Reginald W. Williams Jr.

Introduction

///

Dr. Lani Guinier's book *The Miner's Canary* opens with the description of a miner's canary. It is a startling image of a beautiful bird that is carried by miners into the noxious environment of a mine. Because the canary's fragile respiratory system is much more sensitive than a human's, the toxic fumes in a mine would cause the canary to choke and collapse. Guinier notes that the suffocation of the bird signaled that it was time to leave the mine because existence in the environment was becoming too dangerous. In many ways, oppressed people worldwide are like these suffocating canaries; their distress is too often the first sign of a danger that can soon overwhelm an entire society.

In a cursory assessment, the noxious odors may be perceived as impacting only communities of color. Ignoring such odors, though, can cause an entire society to become vulnerable. This canary metaphor can be expanded beyond those who are marginalized by race to those marginalized by their economic situation, physical appearance, gender, or sexual orientation. With this reality in mind, this book is designed to empower local church ministries to alert their congregations and communities to fumes of oppression before they incapacitate communities of color and cripple God's children at large. For God has created all of God's children as equals.

This is a matter of justice. In his letter from a Birmingham jail, Dr. Martin Luther King Jr., wrote "Injustice anywhere is a threat to justice everywhere."[1] Today social injustice in its many forms plagues the entire planet. Bruce Malchow, in *Social Justice in the Hebrew Bible*, says, "If justice is defined as the quality of being fair and just, then social justice can be defined as the quality of ensuring that fairness and justice are intricately interwoven into each and every aspect of society."[2]

At times the word *injustice* implies illegal acts that deprive people of their rights. However, many recurring unjust acts in the present age are legal, and the present structure of society allows them to recur. People with moral sensitivity recognize that these acts are inherently unfair because they place certain groups at economic or social disadvantage by preventing them from having equal access to basic necessities for life.

Purpose

The first purpose of this book is to be faithful to the call of God in Christ on the church. If we are the church of Jesus Christ, then it only makes sense that God's people emulate the mission and ministry of Christ. That is, the church ought to be about justice because Jesus is about justice. When Jesus preached his first sermon, he quoted Isaiah 61, declaring that "the Spirit of the Lord is upon me because he has anointed me to bring good news to the poor. He has sent me to proclaim release to the captives and recovery of sight to the blind, to let the oppressed go free, to proclaim the year of the Lord's favor" (Luke 4:18-19). Jesus was declaring that he understood himself not only in the line of the prophets but sent to seek justice. When Jesus turned over the tables in the temple, he was upsetting the normal modus operandi of the day, leeching salesmen unfairly profiting off people coming to worship.

If the above is not enough, there are at least two other reasons for a book on social justice ministry. One is to dispel the notion promoted in the mass media that social justice concerns are not to be concerns of the church. As the argument goes, the church should be concerned strictly with the soul's salvation and with ensuring that one is well off financially, mentally, and spiritually regardless of what is taking place in the surrounding world. That is the central message of the so-called prosperity gospel. However, this book concurs with Hank Hanegraaff, in *Christianity in Crisis*, who says that this word of faith/prosperity gospel movement is "a prostitution of the biblical concept of faith and a critical compromise of the respect of the nature of God."[3]

(3) Another purpose of this book is to assist churches with the fight for justice and against that concept of rugged individualism that rejects the notion that we are all inextricably linked to one another. We concur with Dr. Martin Luther King Jr., who said, "We are caught in an inescapable network of mutuality, tied in a single garment of destiny. Whatever affects one directly affects all indirectly."[4] This principle is brought to life further by the South African Bantu principle of Ubuntu, which affirms that I am because we are, and because we are, therefore I am. All of this is because of our relationship one to another and with the God of the universe.

The final purpose of this book brings us back to Dr. Guinier's canary metaphor. It is to provide those who are called by God, laity and clergy alike, with a resource to use in systematically fighting for justice in a context of congregational and community ministry in an unhealthy environment that converges on racial canaries and puts the entire society at risk.

Organization and Content

This book differs from other books on similar topics in that it offers a model and provides specifics for establishing particular components of social justice ministries. It also presents practical guidelines in detail. That is, by establishing the recommended components, churches will be able to create justice ministries tailored for their specific contexts. It is not the intention of this book to dictate what a given church should do within a given church context. It only offers a model or template that can be adapted for various contexts.

Part 1 defines the concept of social justice ministry and also presents its biblical and cultural foundations. Too often social justice ministry is confused with charity, so the information and models in this section are designed to clarify this confusion. We distinguish between ministries of charity alone and the more encompassing concept of social justice ministry.

Part 2 contains a detailed model for implementing justice ministry in the local church and recommends various components to put into practice. The lists contained in this section are not exhaustive. They are based on the authors' experiences as ministers for justice at Friendship-West Baptist Church of Dallas, Texas, the Trinity United Church of Christ in Chicago, and the First Baptist Church of University Park, Illinois. This section provides both tools and tactics. The resource guide contains additional resources for implementing ministries of justice, as well as for educating congregations and communities.

The initial draft of this model has been introduced to people in organizations tangentially related to local churches, including social workers and others. To the extent that any information in this volume is helpful in any other discipline that seeks to change the plight of God's people, God be praised! The prayers behind the development of the book have been that local churches throughout the world will organize justice ministries that benefit the people of God and that "justice will roll down like waters, and righteousness as an ever-flowing stream."[5]

////////

NOTES

1. Martin Luther King, Jr., *Letter from a Birmingham Jail,* April 16, 1963, www.africa.upenn.edu/Articles_Gen/Letter_Birmingham.html (accessed October 4, 2012).

2. Bruce V. Malchow, *Social Justice in the Hebrew Bible* (Nashville: Thomas Nelson, 1996), 38.

3. Hank Hanegraaff, *Chrisitianity in Crisis* (Nashville: Thomas Nelson, 2009), ix.

4. Martin Luther King Jr., *Letter from a Birmingham Jail,* April 16, 1963, www.africa.upenn.edu/Articles_Gen/Letter_Birmingham.html (accessed October 4, 2012).

5. Martin Luther King Jr., address delivered to the Southern Christian Leadership Conference, *"Where Do We Go From Here,"* August 16, 1967.

Getting on Board

CHAPTER 1
Understanding Social Justice Ministry

From the outset we need to recognize that social justice ministry is much broader than charity alone. Thinking of social justice as charity alone is a common misunderstanding. This confusion was exemplified when a professor expressed interest in bringing their class to observe social justice ministry at the church where Rev. Williams served from 2002–2008, Trinity United Church of Christ. The social justice ministry at Trinity UCC was comprised of 13 different ministries which engaged in not only meeting persons needs, but also challenging policies which made those needs possible in the first place. For instance, the Housing Ministry, one of the 13 justice ministries, not only assisted persons in preparation to become homeowners, but they also challenged negative policies in the city and county regarding home ownership, red-lining, etc. The model was not only to meet needs but to challenge policies that made needs possible. Another example was the HIV/AIDS ministry. This ministry provided safe space for those affected and infected by HIV/AIDS. Additionally, this ministry challenged policies, which did not make anti-retroviral drugs affordable to those who desperately needed access. Again, the model was not only to meet needs, but also to challenge policies, which made needs possible. As our dialogue progressed and I attempted to explain that our social justice ministries not only ministered to the person but also challenged the systems that created the person's need for justice, the professor asked whether our church ran a soup kitchen or had a clothing give-away warehouse. Rev. Williams responded that we did engage in food and clothing distribution. However the church does not have a soup kitchen, nor a clothing warehouse. The professor was disappointed and seemed confused, because to the professor, those ministries of charity were ministries of justice. This professor is not alone in that confusion. This book dispels the notion that charity, of itself, completes the definition of social justice ministry. Charity and justice, while linked, are two separate entities. One need only look to the definitions of the two terms to see a difference in meaning. Below is the dictionary entry for *charity* from the *Merriam-Webster Online Dictionary.*

> char·i·ty: (1) benevolent goodwill toward or love of humanity; (2) a: generosity and helpfulness especially toward the needy or suffering; *also* aid given to those in need; b: an institution engaged in relief of the poor; c: public provision for the relief of the needy; (3) a: a gift for public benevolent purposes; b: an institution (as a hospital) founded by such a gift; (4) lenient judgment of others.

The English word *charity* traces its etymological origins through Anglo-French to the Latin *caritas*, meaning "Christian love." Now compare and contrast the definition of *charity* with the definition of *justice* from the same dictionary.

> jus·tice: (1) a: the maintenance or administration of what is just, especially by the impartial adjustment of conflicting claims or the assignment of merited rewards or punishments; b: judge; c: the administration of law; especially the establishment or determination of rights according to the rules of law or equity; (2) a: the quality of being just, impartial, or fair; b: (i) the principle or ideal of just dealing or right action; (ii) conformity to this principle or ideal: righteousness; c: the quality of conforming to law; (3) conformity to truth, fact, or reason: CORRECTNESS.

As with *charity,* the etymology of *justice* is traced via Anglo-French from the Latin *justitia,* which is derived from *justus.*

When we view both definitions, it is clear that despite some similarities, marked differences exist. Charity, as defined, gives a sense of generosity and benevolence to a soul in need. In his book, *Urban Churches, Vital Signs: Beyond Charity toward Justice*, Nile Harper says, "Charity is understood to be works of love, acts of mutual aid, the duty of Christians. . . . This perspective emphasizes personal deeds of mercy and acts of compassion within the local community."[1] Charity essentially becomes a reaction in order to supply a need based on some lack in another's life. Charity is essential but of itself is not adequate for meeting the person's need or the needs of the group that person represents.

In contrast, justice seeks to maintain a system of equality without partiality. That is, it seeks right treatment. Unlike charity alone, justice is not limited to reacting in order to fulfill a material need such as food. Justice seeks right systemic relationships from the get-go. That is, "social justice focuses on basic causes of oppression, inequity, and disenfranchisement. It seeks to change public policy and public priorities. It works to empower people to take initiatives in ways that are positive and constructive. The movement for social justice understands that oppressed people have strengths, skills, cultural assets, and the responsibility to act corporately for their own common good."[2] Where charity is reactive to specific material needs, justice is more proactive, working for changes in systems that create such needs.

For example, in the example of the soup kitchen, charity is offered by volunteers who donate ingredients, prepare the soup, and serve the poor and homeless. Physical bodies are being nourished. It is true that stomachs knotted by hunger pangs need to be fed. Justice, however, asks why anyone is hungry in the wealthiest country in the world. Justice education exposes and seeks to address the ways in which hunger interfaces with issues such as poverty and redistribution of wealth. It uncovers and works against capitalistic manipulations in favor of the privileged that lead to the hunger of the poor.

Another illustration that helps to clarify the difference between charity and justice is one that quite frequently is presented from pulpits to illustrate a social justice mission of a given church: a thermometer reacts to the circumstances around it, but a thermostat sets the temperature for the circumstances around it. The thermometer represents charity, which reacts to what is going on around it. For example, the more the economy shifts downward, the more soup kitchens will open to feed the increasing numbers of jobless and homeless people. However, while charity merely reacts to its environment, justice, like a thermostat, acts to *change* the environment. Justice seeks to adjust the social and political environment to eliminate the need for soup kitchens in the first place. Justice work—like a thermostat—places pressure on politicians and policy makers to ensure that none of God's children are too hot from the heat of oppressive measures or too cold from the wintry chill of political and societal rejection.

Archbishop Dom Helder Camara (1902–1999), who founded the Banco da Providencia in Rio De Janeira in 1959 (a philanthropic organization which fights poverty) and served as Roman Catholic Archbishop, brings both of these separate yet related themes to bear when he asks, "When I give food to the poor, they call me a saint. When I ask why they are poor, they call me a Communist."[3] The archbishop's concern is still valid even years after his death. Oppressors are comfortable with charitable organizations and individuals. Those in power generally do not mind having those in need assisted. However, when one challenges the systems that make charity necessary, problems arise. The work of justice challenges the privilege and power of those who don't mind "throwing a few crumbs" of charity but refuse to establish systems of equality, mutuality, reciprocity, and impartiality.

Both charity and justice are essential to the work of churches, but an exclusive focus on charity impedes progress toward justice. An exclusive focus on charity can cause people to accept things as they are and never seek the changes that justice provides, changes that ultimately make charity unnecessary. Until the day comes when charity becomes unnecessary, however, a concerted effort must be made that includes both charity and justice. Churches do not have the luxury of forsaking justice for charity or forsaking charity for justice. Social justice ministries must employ both in order to bring about a world where God's people will be treated as God would have them be treated. Social justice is not to be confused with social services. Social services are charitable services that are responsive to individual needs and require repetition. Social justice can be defined as public and group acts that offer permanent relief. The contrast between social service and social justice can be seen by looking at Luke 10 and Exodus 3. In Luke 10:25-37, Jesus told the story of a good Samaritan who assisted a beaten traveler along the road. He soothed the victim's wounds with olive oil and wine, bandaged him, and provided temporary shelter. The traveler indeed felt better due to the selfless and generous service rendered by the good Samaritan; however, the good Samaritan did not address the root cause of why the traveler was beaten, battered, and bruised. The good Samaritan is an example of performing social service. This is the challenge with many of the efforts in our communities and even our churches. Too often we engage only in social services, which amounts to charity, but rarely move further to address root causes which lead to justice. Therefore this same scenario could have happened again to the next traveler, if the root cause of the beating, battering, and bruising is never addressed. It is the equivalent of giving a cancer patient an aspirin for temporary relief of pain, but never getting to addressing the cancer.

In contrast, Exodus 3:10 records that Moses, having spent time on the "back side of the mountain," was directed to go directly to Pharoah. In other words, he was sent to the entity which made policy decisions on how people are treated. Upon arriving before the seat of power and policy, Moses did not ask for more humane treatment in a sick system of slavery. In Exodus 5, he confronted Pharaoh and said the time for oppression was over and to let God's people go! Moses aimed to destroy the oppressive system of slavery that would have created the need for social services.

Biblical Foundations for Social Justice Ministry

The Bible addresses social justice from Genesis through Revelation as a requirement of faithful service to God. Nowhere is this as clear as in Micah 6:8: "What does the LORD require of you but to do justice, and to love kindness, and to walk humbly with your God?"

Rev. Dr. Jerome C. Ross, pastor of the Providence Park Baptist Church in Richmond, Virginia, and former associate professor of Old Testament at the Samuel DeWitt Proctor School of Theology at Virginian Union University, helps us to see the social situation of the ancient Yahwists and the conditions under which they lived. He says, "Except for the reign of David–Solomon, the Yahwists were dominated by the superpower nations during the biblical period."[4] Then and now, living under oppression means at least four things: (1) forced acceptance of administrative arrangements, (2) payment of taxes, (3) forced acceptance of the oppressor's religion and their characterization of what should be the oppressed religion, and (4) unconditional loyalty (no foreign alliances).[5]

The Bible shows the Israelites living under oppression of six empires: Egyptian, Assyrian, Babylonian, Persian, Greek, and Roman. Under these the people were not free to determine their own way of being. In these contexts they lived to survive. Their need for survival forced the question, in the words of Dr. John Henrik Clarke, "How will my people stay on this earth?"[6]

Further, according to Jerome Ross, the extent to which they survived depended on seven factors: (1) administrative structure, (2) economic independence, (3) ideological standardization (laws or rules for a given community), (4) common language, (5) the selective appropriation of the dominant culture, (6) people or population, and (7) land. (When these seven critical factors were viewed in Bible class at First Baptist Church of University Park, the class came up with an eighth factor: healthy self-identity!) The extent to which a people may be able to control these factors or have these factors controlled by other entities such as governmental agencies or corporate elites, another, according to Ross, determines the extent of a people's freedom. Under these varied types of oppression and domination, Ross says, "the primary concern that is reflected in the Bible is the survival of a minority. That is, the quest for preservation and perpetuation of community identity or meaningful existence by a people who are not fully self determinant."[7]

Beginning this book with this outlook is important, because traditional Christianity has taught for so long that what takes place on Sunday morning and what happens Monday through Saturday were separate. That is, what happens inside of the church and outside of the church had nothing to do with one another. For so long, churches have taught that the Bible should only govern how a person lives day to day. However, Ross's research shows that this dichotomy is not real. In fact, when biblical texts are examined from the perspective of the systemic oppressions the Israelites faced, the entire text is seen differently and thus ought to be interpreted differently than traditional ways based on white supremacy and hegemony. Ross draws parallels between the people of God in the biblical text and the people of African descent living in America. This outlook provides biblical support for the fight for freedom from any powers or principalities that oppress or overrun people. It provides a different framework for preaching, teaching, and reaching out into churches and communities.

In the Bible, one can see that the objective of most Israelite social justice programs was to aid the most vulnerable and unprotected in society. There was a particular concern for widows, orphans, resident aliens, laborers, peasant farmers, and beggars. They were to be cared for through legal systems, governing authorities, and temple programs. These institutions were expected to be just, fair, and equitable. The Hebrew Bible translates *justice* using the Hebrew term *mishpat*. *Mishpat* indicates that every member of the community had rights due to them based simply on their humanity. The goal for justice was to promote equity and restore community harmony as it related to particular situations or environments.

Beginning with the law codes, inclusive of the Book of the Covenant (Exodus 20:22–23:33), Deuteronomic code (Deuteronomy 12–26), and the holiness code (Leviticus 17–26), laws for the community were ascribed to and accepted. They called for the care and concern of the entire community. Generally, mistreatment was prohibited. More often than not, however, special care was given to the most vulnerable of society—those who were widowed and orphaned. These laws called for both fair treatment and love. They expressly forbade actions that would exploit the poor. Economic parity, sharing of resources, fair treatment in courts, and love of neighbor as self were laws set down in an effort to establish a just society.

In addition to the law codes, the prophets spoke about the need for social justice. During times when justice was perverted by the rich to the detriment of the poor (just as it is today), the prophets spoke truth about moral abuses that "pimped" the poor but preserved privilege for the rich and wealthy. Many of the prophets spoke about very specific instances of injustice. For example, Amos spoke about the bitterness of the injustices of the rich oppressing the poor by violating laws that were intended to protect the poor (just as Tea Party members, social conservatives, and immoral members of the judicial branch of government do today; see Exodus 22:26, Amos 2:8). Another example is Ezekiel, who spoke specifically about how the poor were charged interest for loans, just as borrowers who use payday loan parlors are charged exorbitant interest rates today (Ezekiel 18:5, 7-8). Isaiah also wrote a scathing critique of those who denied justice to the needy and deprived them of their rights, especially widows and orphans (Isaiah 1:17, Isaiah 58:1-14). All of the prophets addressed themes of justice and injustice.

Throughout the book of Psalms—the hymnbook of the Hebrew people—and the Wisdom literature—Job, Proverbs, and Ecclesiastes—songs are sung and sayings are spoken that reveal the need for social justice. One only needs to hear the words of Psalm 137 to hear the cry of God's people for justice: "By the rivers of Babylon—there we sat down and there we wept when we remembered Zion" (v. 1). Many of the psalms arose out of a context of oppression with the writers asking God to avenge them against their oppressors. The Wisdom literature speaks consistently about the wisdom of treating the poor with dignity and respect. Proverbs 22:22 admonishes the people not to "rob the poor because they are poor or crush the afflicted at the gate." Moreover, Wisdom literature expressly opposes unjust actions toward the poor and even offers the consequences of injustice being levied against them. However, Wisdom literature also prescribes actions to be taken by the poor to engage in social justice wisely. It speaks both of people and governments. Proverbs 29:7, for example, deals with the fair treatment of the poor. Proverbs 29:14 states that if a king deals rightly with the poor, then his throne will be established forever.

The Gospels of the New Testament show Jesus, Lord and Savior, coming in both the tradition and line of the prophets, speaking and preaching about the abuses of the powerful against the powerless. In fact, when Jesus preached his first sermon, he took his text from the scroll of the prophet Isaiah (Isaiah 61). Luke 4:18-19 records Jesus as saying, "The Spirit of the Lord is upon me, because he has anointed me to bring good news to the poor. He has sent me to proclaim release to the captives and recovery of sight to the blind, to let the oppressed go free, to proclaim the year of the Lord's favor." Jesus then said, "Today this scripture has been fulfilled in your hearing" (v. 21). In other words, Jesus said that this word had been made flesh! Poverty, incarceration, health care, and societal oppression were issues that were in the Master's mission statement. Moreover, Jesus said that he understood his calling to address these issues that had plagued God's people. Very plainly, Jesus understood himself as being sent in the tradition of the prophets. Apparently he saw his mission of seeking and fighting for justice for God's people.

The apostle Paul is also seen fighting for social justice in his epistles. He championed the role of women in a society that treated them as property and not as people. Throughout the Pauline epistles we can find the themes of equality, mutuality, and reciprocity. Thomas Hoyt, in *True to Our Native Land*, suggests that Paul offers a formula for the mixture of Christians and politics and tells how believers can make the state better. He says that we must: "(1) desire peace, justice, and order in accordance with God's purpose for God's creation; and (2) concern [ourselves with] that which fosters harmony and unity in the church so that the church may carry out its redemptive mission." Hoyt interprets Paul as saying that these concerns, "rather than a blind, unconditional commitment to any and every civil authority, should guide our attitude toward authorities."[8] In the book of Revelation, one finds John the revelator exiled on an island called Patmos. He is seen revealing to the churches what God has to say about the treatment of those who have been slaughtered by oppressive systems and governments. He sets forth the vision that God will be victorious over such evil after all. These are just a few biblical snapshots that reveal common threads of social justice and that support the need for social justice ministries.

Social Justice in the Historic African American Church

Dr. Harry S. Wright, former Dean of Chapel at the now defunct Bishop College in Dallas, Texas, preached a sermon in the summer of 2010 at Friendship-West Baptist Church in Dallas titled "A Reminder." He opened his sermon by saying, "I will be preaching from Joshua 4, but I will not read it. I am simply going to drop my anchor there." In that same spirit, as authors of this book, will not attempt to recount the entire history of the black church's legacy of engaging in social justice. Like Dr. Wright, we simply want to drop our anchor in a storied past replete with movements that demonstrate the power of the black church's pursuit of social justice. We are reminded of the struggles, strides, and successes of the black church impact on this nation. The aftermath of the "peculiar institution" has and continues to inform the construction of public policy and to guide how individuals interact with those inside and outside their race. Hopefully this brief outline will become the beginning of explorations into the contributions of these historic justice fighters. Their lives and collective movements can be taught and used as inspiration for continuing the struggle for social justice in the twenty-first century. The black church has endured by rendering both social service and social justice. It has survived physically, mentally, and spiritually because of prophetic ministers and laypersons. Backed by the church, many stood in opposition to a hostile government, rejected unjust policies, and lived out Micah's decree to do justice, love mercy, and walk humbly before the Almighty against great odds. Traditionally the black church has served as the conscience of the state and the lifeline of the community. Even as far back as the days when slavery was common in the southern United States, the church was at the center of the slave community. And today the African American church still remains the most organized, visible, and nurturing institution for the overall life of black North Americans.

Dr. Martin Luther King Jr. and Fannie Lou Hamer stood courageously before this nation, challenging it to be true to its founding principles recorded in the Declaration of Independence "that all men are created equal, that they are endowed by their Creator with certain unalienable Rights, that among these are Life, Liberty and the pursuit of Happiness." They both spoke truth to power and people in such a way that the Civil Rights Act of 1964 and the Voting Rights Act of 1965 were passed into law and the white power structure in the state of Mississippi was exposed for its oppressive and violent actions that disenfranchised black citizens.

At its inception, the black church served as a haven for worshipping God in spirit and in truth and as a statement against the slaveholder's version of worship. It gave us spiritual strength to face our social situation. Africans slipped down into the brush arbor to worship the God they knew before arriving on the shores of North America. The cross was and continues to be at the heart of the black church. The cross for the slaves represented the story of Jesus as a liberator. This is a story of suffering, rebellion, and ultimately victory. Victory even in bondage was obtainable.

Moreover, it is a story that details the fact that their religion was not bound to what people could do to them physically. A day might bring severe punishment via the "cat-o'-nine-tails," "death by noose," branding, or being sold off, never to see loved ones again. But victory was won, even when it looked like they lost in the natural. Second Corinthians 5:1 says that "if the earthly tent we live in is destroyed, we have a building from God, a house not made with hands, eternal in the heavens." For the enslaved, on the other side of the cross was the resurrection and Christ. This is why they sang this song:

> Befo' I be a slave
> I'll be buried in my grave
> and go home to my Lord
> and be free.

Furthermore, they believed Philippians 1:21, which says, "living is Christ and dying is gain." On the slaves' long walk to freedom, they believed in a God who never left them alone in their plea for freedom.

The black church, in slavery, recognized the relationship between being Christian and engaging in social struggle. In fact, it was their relationship with God that gave them the strength to struggle. They also understood that they were duty bound to disobey the state's actions that contradicted divine law and order. Harriet Tubman understood that a human being was born free and that no person could give or take freedom. Life and freedom were God's alone to give. So she went against the state-sanctioned system of slavery and became the conductor of the Underground Railroad. She rendered a social service by ushering hundreds of passengers up North and into Canada to freedom. Her actions, in part, set the stage for permanent change to occur, in the form of the Emancipation Proclamation.

Rev. Nat Turner engaged in confrontation to end the dark days of slavery. Sojourner Truth was a preacher, abolitionist, and womanist. Traveling across New England, she preached a prophetic and liberating word, connecting the dots of race, class, and gender in the fight against human oppression. Shortly after the Emancipation Proclamation, a short-lived era known as Reconstruction emerged. Reconstruction can be characterized as an era in American history when the nation as a whole was rebuilding from the Civil War and the South (Confederacy) was being transformed due in part to newly freed slaves who made gains economically, socially, and politically. Bishop Henry McNeal Turner served in the Georgia House of Representatives. Rev. Hiram Rhodes Revels became the first black senator from Mississippi. He stood for justice. In fact, his first speech from the Senate floor was a plea for black legislators in the state of Georgia. Phillip Dray writes in *Capitol Men*, "Revels challenged the readmission of Georgia to the Union on the grounds that the state had denied blacks the right to serve in its legislature and had indeed a year and a half earlier expelled those already serving."[9]

Contemporaries Ida. B. Wells-Barnett and Mary McLeod Bethune both initiated movements out of their faith. Wells, using the power of the pen, set off a local and national debate surrounding the lynching of blacks, specifically black men who became the center point of Billie Holiday's recording "Strange Fruit." Wells published *A Red Record* that documented lynchings, and she became the leader of the antilynching crusade. In 1889 Wells became a partner in the *Free Speech and Headlight*, a black-owned Memphis newspaper. Rev. R. Nightingale, the pastor of Beale Street Baptist Church, often encouraged his congregation to support the paper. Eventually Wells was able to work full-time for the paper and buy out Nightingale. She also taught Sunday school. Her outspoken nature often put her in harms way as she confronted white supremacy.

Bethune was born into a farming family in Mayesville, South Carolina, where she maintained her faith in God and believed in the power of education. There are times when one must confront systematic injustices, and then there are times when one must parallel that struggle with efforts to create a new system. Bethune posited that "educated black women should assume the burden to uplift their families by providing moral, Christian leadership at home and in their communities."[10] She founded what would eventually become Bethune-Cookman College, a school that offered educational opportunities for black people. Another example of a time when it was necessary to confront injustice was the Birmingham bus boycott, which was led by Dr. Martin Luther King Jr. and was made successful by the community of faith. It was a demonstration of how a movement rooted in the church could break the backbone of Jim Crow segregation. Reverend Vernon Johns towered above his time. Using the pulpit at Dexter Avenue Baptist Church, Johns preached collective economic empowerment and liberation, laying the foundation for Dr. Martin Luther King Jr.

Freedom Summer

The moving spirit of continuing the fight for freedom, justice, and equality found its way down to the Mississippi Delta in 1964. The summer project was designed to set up freedom schools to address the inferior public education of black children. The catalyst for the movement was registering blacks to vote and exposing the oppressive structures that precluded blacks from participating in the democratic process. Many of the volunteers consisted of northern white college students and brave blacks in Mississippi. Some lost their lives. Most notably, Andrew Goodman, Michael Schwerner, and James Chaney died a terrible death while seeking justice, while others such as Fannie Lou Hamer suffered beatings almost unto death. Hamer emerged as a hero that summer. She presented her body as a living sacrifice, risking loss of shelter, the breaking of family bonds, and living under constant death threats. Emboldened by her faith, she delivered a televised testimony on behalf of the Mississippi Freedom Democratic Party. Her actions and sacrifices, in part, set the stage for the Voting Rights Act of 1965.

Consistent with this strong tradition, we must elect leaders with a strong faith tradition and/or highly principled leaders, and we must serve as a moral influence in society. We are duty bound to make the state better.

Oppression of the Poor Today

When it comes to treatment of the poor, parallels between ancient and modern societies are apparent. The most vulnerable in society are still being overlooked and exploited. Poor people are still being targeted for unfair loans with exorbitant interest rates. Poor people are still being denied the most basic of human rights. Poor people are not even on the radar when it comes to political policy decisions, and rarely are the poor discussed in political campaigns. Social justice is still not a reality!

Consider the following chart, which provides information from the U.S. Census Bureau on the threshold of poverty in the United States.

2009 Poverty Thresholds, Selected Family Types[11]

	AGE	INCOME LEVEL
Single Individual	Under 65 years	$11,161
	65 years & older	$10,289
Single Parent	1 child	$14,787
	2 children	$17,285
Two Adults	No children	$14,366
	1 child	$17,268
	2 children	$21,756
	3 children	$25,603

Given the thresholds listed above, consider the number of children (the future) who live in poverty. Children are 25 percent of the total population yet 35 percent of the population of those living in poverty. "In 2008, 15.45 million children, or 20.7 percent, were poor. The poverty rate for children also varies substantially by race and Hispanic origin."[12] (See the following table.)

Children under 18 Living in Poverty, 2008[13]

CATEGORY	NUMBER (in thousands)	PERCENT
All children under 18	15,451	20.7
White only, non-Hispanic	4,850	11.9
Black	4,480	35.4
Hispanic	5,610	33.1
Asian	531	13.3

The poor, those whom Jesus called "the least of these," are not properly cared for today. As the proliferation of mass incarceration continues to spread in this era of "the New Jim Crow,"[14] the poor are attacked and targeted more in an effort to service this sick system.

America, the richest country in the world, throws away food that could feed the hungry. According to Bread for the World, one in every eight people in America lives below the federal poverty line.[15] For African Americans, that number is one in every four.[16] These numbers also reflect the number of households who struggle to place food on the table daily while average American families throw away food worth over $165 billion annually, or 20 pounds of food per person per month.[17] That may not sound like much, but table scraps to some are banquets to others. "In 1997, in one of the few studies of food waste, the Department of Agriculture estimated that two years before, 96.4 billion pounds of the 356 billion pounds of edible food in the United States was [sic] never eaten. Fresh produce, milk, grain products and sweeteners made up two-thirds of the waste. An update is under way."[18]

In the state of Texas, some financial institutions carry out their lending practices through a loophole. This loophole enables the business to engage in lending practices without following or complying with state laws. We refer to these businesses as legalized loan sharks or predatory lenders. Unfortunately, in some economically distressed communities there is a proliferation of payday and auto title loan stores. Many vulnerable citizens turn to these businesses to secure a short-term loan that may range from $100 to $500 at an interest rate as high as 700 percent. The payment is due within two weeks. If the borrower is unable to pay, they incur a rollover fee that extends the loan for another two weeks. Many borrowers are in desperate situations. Some need money to pay the rent or mortgage, buy medication, care for grandchildren, or for some other necessity. In a sense, predatory lenders take advantage of this desperation by charging excessive fees and employing intimidating collection practices. Most borrowers find themselves deeper in debt with no way out. For that reason, during a Sunday morning worship service, Rev. Dr. Frederick D. Haynes III made it a point to lay out the problem with predatory lending in the community and made the linkage to what our faith tradition teaches about usury. More details on this movement to change public policy on predatory lending are discussed in chapter 4. This is an example of the tradition of prophetic ministry and social justice addressing the needs of the poor as they exist today.

The Need for Social Justice Ministries Today

Yesterday the truth of unjust policies in the social order was much more obvious. The noose, the whip, the branding iron, the billy club, the water hose, and the dogs were clearly visible. The threat was immediate. Today the signs of injustice are obvious though a bit more veiled. If we take the time to look and be aware, we will see that forms of dehumanization, though different, still exist. Symbols of power and domination can, for example, be found in degenerative public policies, lack of city services, little to no code enforcement, construction of concrete jungles, inferior schools, excessive unemployment, and the war on drugs. These elements are designed to impose humiliation on, strike fear into, and control the population who live on the margins. This sets an atmosphere for people to self-destruct. We ask how long we can sit in an "airtight cage of poverty in the midst of an affluent society."[19]

We are presented with challenges in the form of globalization, assaults on collective bargaining, mass incarceration, labor migration, deregulation of industries, outsourcing, and the fight for workers' rights. In the winter of 2011, the Wisconsin Assembly passed a bill that essentially stripped the majority of public workers of their collective bargaining rights. The March 11, 2011, tsunami in Japan resulted in U.S.-based Toyota factories temporarily canceling overtime to conserve inventory supplied by Japan, according to a *USA Today* news article.[20]

The voice of the faith community must be heard. The challenge facing the black church and anyone pursuing social justice is how to organize and mobilize during the time of the first elected person of African descent. There is a myth that the country has entered a postracial society. Therefore, it is also being said that the country no longer has institutional and social barriers that preclude citizens, primarily minorities, from achieving "the American Dream." However, one need only survey America's inner cities or the southern sector of Dallas, Texas, or University Park, Illinois, where food deserts[21] exist, lack of sustainable economic development is prevalent, residents are subjected to inferior city services, and a proliferation of payday and auto title loan businesses operate as legalized loan sharks. An unbiased assessment would conclude that the struggle against oppression continues. It is still necessary for the church to engage in public policy and help guide political discourse. It is in this area that decisions must be made as to how resources will be allocated and what groups are deserving of those resources.

The church must continue to ask itself, what is the mission of the church, and of the black church? It is imperative that the church be keenly aware of the times in which it is living. It is possible to "do the right thing," but if at the wrong time, it may be ineffective. The church is called to save both bodies and souls. When a pastor stands before a congregation on Sunday morning and has a political message or interjects a sociopolitical view, it is a signal that a tension exists between the state and the divine order.

The legacy the church has inherited demands that as a collection of Christians we engage in social justice.[22] Nothing is more important than living out that calling on the life and mission of the church. The church must do this in the face of the reality that many people of this nation find themselves trapped in a cycle of chronic unemployment and underemployment. We find ourselves with inadequate health care or no health care, with failing public schools, with distressed communities devoid of substantive and sustainable economic development. We find ourselves with unbalanced food diets characterized by the lack of access to fresh produce. The list goes on. We hope this book will offer a framework for those who wish to join God in setting such captives free.

////////

NOTES

1. Nile Harper, *Urban Churches, Vital Signs: Beyond Charity toward Justice* (Grand Rapids and Cambridge, UK: Eerdmans, 1999), 298.

2. Ibid., 300.

3. See http://www.goodreads.com/quotes/show/20321.

4. Jerome Clayton Ross, "The Cultural Affinity between the Ancient Yahwists and the African Americans: A Hermeneutic for Homiletics," in Samuel K. Roberts, ed., *Born to Preach: Essays in Honor of the Ministry of Henry and Ella Mitchell* (Valley Forge, PA: Judson, 2000), 22.

5. Ibid., 23.

6. Wesley Snipes (Producer). *John Henrik Clarke: A Great and Mighty Walk* (DVD/VHS) (Black Dot Media: Hollywood, CA, 1996).

7. Ross, "Cultural Affinity between the Ancient Yahwists and the African Americans," 27.

8. Thomas Hoyt, quoted in Brian K. Blount, Cain Hope Felder, Clarice J. Martin, and Emerson B. Powery, *True to Our Native Land* (Minneapolis: Fortress, 2007), 270.

9. Philip Dray, *Capitol Men: The Epic Story of Reconstruction through the Lives of the First Black Congressmen* (Boston and New York: Houghton Mifflin, 2008), 73.

10. McClusky, Audrey Thomas and Smith, Elaine M. *Mary McLeod Bethune: Building A Better World* (Bloomington, IN, Indiana University Press, 2001), p. 5

11. *Income, Poverty, and Health Insurance Coverage in the United States: 2009*, U.S. Department of Commerce, U.S. Bureau of the Census, Report P60, n. 238, p. 55.

12. See http://www.npc.umich.edu/poverty/#_ftn4. The Census now allows people to report more than one race. In this table, black includes anyone who reported black, whether or not they also reported another racial identity. The same is true for Asian. Hispanics can be of any race because that label is a cultural one, related to language more than to ethnicity. The numbers for

each subgroup do not add up exactly to the total, because subtotals for some groups, including Native Americans and Pacific Islanders, are not available in the census report.

13. *Income, Poverty, and Health Insurance Coverage in the United States: 2009*, n. 238, Table B-2, 62–67.

14. Michelle Alexander. *The New Jim Crow: Mass Incarceration in the Age of Colorblindness* (New York and London: New Press, 2010).

15. *Income, Poverty, and Health Insurance Coverage in the United States: 2008*, U.S. Department of Commerce, U.S. Census Bureau, September 2009, Table 4, http://www.census.gov/prod/2010pubs/p60-238.pdf.

16. Ibid.

17. See http://www.huffingtonpost.com/2012/08/21/food-waste-americans-throw-away-food-study_n_1819340.html. "As a country, we're essentially tossing every other piece of food that crosses our path. That's money and precious resources down the drain," said Dana Gunders, a scientist with the Natural Resources Defense Council's food and agriculture program.

18. Andrew Martin, "One Country's Table Scraps, Another Country's Meal," *New York Times*, May 18, 2008, WK3.

19. James M. Washington, ed., *I Have a Dream: Writings and Speeches that Changed the World* (New York: Harper Collins, 1992), 88.

20. R. James Healey. Toyota Cancels Overtime in U.S. to Conserve Parts, *USA Today*, March 14, 2011, www.usatoday.com/communities/driveon/post/2011/03/tsunami-cancels-toyota-overtime-in-us-threatens-supplies-of-luxury-and-high-mileage-models-.1#.UKJOOHy9KK0

21. In the 2008 Farm Bill, *food desert* is defined as an "area in the United States with limited access to affordable and nutritious food, particularly such an area composed of predominantly lower income neighborhoods and communities" (Title VI, sec. 7527).

22. This legacy is fully addressed in the book by L. H. Whelchel Jr., *History and Heritage of African American Churches: A Way Out of No Way* (St. Paul: Paragon, 2011).

CHAPTER 2

Discovering the Power of Relationships

Ministries of justice within the church should be internally based and externally relevant. For this to be accomplished, ministries of justice must be comprised of several components of engagement. This chapter focuses on how such components can manifest as justice ministry, beginning within the local church. It stresses how to incorporate the care of souls, educate both church and community, interact with individuals and organizations, and take collective political action.

Internal

Care of the soul involves helping to meet people's holistic needs. We must not be concerned only about a person's spiritual salvation; we must be concerned with all of a person's needs. In other words, it is futile to tell a person who is physically hungry about personal salvation if you aren't trying to meet the person's need to eat! When a person is hungry, the only thing he or she cares about is having the need for nutritional sustenance met. Without it, they won't hear anything anyway. Providing such a need speaks to what Jesus said in Matthew 25: "For I was hungry and you gave me food, I was thirsty and you gave me something to drink. . . . Just as you did it to one of the least of these who are members of my family, you did it to me" (vv. 35, 40). It is the care of the soul by way of caring for the physical body that is on the charity side of social justice work. Care of the soul is essential.

Education of the congregation and community seeks to apprise people of important facts, issues, and statistics related to specific justice issues. Such education is not only empowering, but when the community and church are well-informed about what is taking place around them, their anxiety and dissent are alleviated. That is why education ought to move the congregation and community to a higher level of *political awareness, organized advocacy, and action.* Action can include boycotts, letter-writing campaigns, visits to elected officials' offices, and/or visits to corporate boardrooms. There is no substitute for action!

The church must be willing to collaborate with other ministries and organizations to further the cause of justice. These *collaborations* are essential. As an African proverb says, "Together the ants ate the elephant," which simply means that one ant cannot kill an elephant alone, but together, many ants can kill and eat the elephant. This is true, especially with regard to faith communities. Denominational and interfaith lines must be crossed in order to make a difference in the lives of affected people.

Case Study: HIV/AIDS Ministry

Ministries of justice are created and implemented around needs that are present in the church itself or in the community. Therefore creating a ministry of justice around HIV/AIDS signifies that the parish recognizes that this ministry is necessary. This may seem obvious, but there are those who still believe that HIV/AIDS is a curse from God to be visited upon sinners (i.e., same-gender-loving individuals). The fact is, HIV/AIDS is a global pandemic. For example, 5 percent of people living in sub-Saharan Africa are infected. Further, according to AVERT, an international HIV and AIDS charity based in the UK working to avert HIV and AIDS worldwide through education, treatment and care, approximately 34 million people worldwide were living with HIV/AIDS in

2010.[1] In the United States, by race, Blacks/African Americans face the most severe burden of HIV.[2] The question is, what would a ministry of justice centered around HIV/AIDS look like? The possibilities can be visualized using the lenses of the components mentioned above.

Care of the Soul

Too often, because of ignorance, persons living with HIV/AIDS are cast outside of the warm womb of the community as though they are the lepers of biblical days. Care of the soul for the person with HIV/AIDS means treating that individual as a person and not a problem. That may mean establishing support groups for people with HIV/AIDS so that they might support one another. Another manner of caring for the soul may be incorporating those living with HIV/AIDS into the active life of the congregation through programming and personal contact. These actions will provide affirmation and ensure that there is at least one place—the church—where, regardless of one's condition, a person can feel like she or he matters. This ministry of affirmation is essential in ministering to the person and caring for the soul.

Education of the Congregation and Community

Education about HIV/AIDS must include distinguishing between facts and falsehoods both about the disease and about its contagion. Rev. Dr. Jeremiah Wright has stated on more than one occasion from the pulpit of Trinity United Church of Christ that HIV/AIDS is spread in three ways: (1) blood, (2) semen, and (3) ignorance. Therefore, education of the congregation and community is an effort to eliminate the third manner of transmission. This in turn can have an effect on the former two manners of transmission.

Transmission is not the only subject matter for education, however. Information is also needed on the disproportionately high rates at which black and poor people are impacted by the disease. This knowledge is essential in African American churches.

Education is also needed on the worldwide fight against HIV/ AIDS, particularly as it relates to antiretroviral drugs that can help prolong the life of persons affected by this disease.

In South Africa, for example, cocktails of generic antiretroviral medications are available for approximately $30 per month. In Brazil, because the government sees the importance of stemming the tide of the HIV/AIDS pandemic, antiretrovirals are free. However, in the United States, costs for even generic drugs are astronomical, and the drugs are often inaccessible to the poor. (This speaks to another issue that needs to continue to be addressed by the church—the health care system and access to health care in the United States.)

Political Action and Awareness

Education should lead to awareness and action. The time is far past for the church only to speak about what is wrong and do nothing about it. Action should always be preceded by education so that one is fighting with the proper tools. One tool a ministry of justice may use to fight against HIV/AIDS is letters, written not only to elected officials but also to corporate executives, business leaders, and others who are deemed the "powers that be."

Demonstrations are another form of action against HIV/AIDS. Letters are good, but bodies attached to letters are better. Experience has taught that letters accompanied by physical presence show the importance of the letters being carried. Other means of action include phone calls and rallies. The point is not the type of action but that some action takes place.

Collaboration

Justice ministries must be willing to go outside the walls of the church. Too often church members remain within little fiefdoms and become territorial over issues that affect all people. But there is truth to the old adage that there is strength in numbers.

With the rate at which HIV/AIDS is attacking people, ministries of justice must be willing to collaborate with other organizations, ministries, and entities to make a difference in slowing down this pandemic. A good national organization to partner with is the Balm in Gilead Foundation.[3] No organization has all information and resources needed. But with each organization and ministry bringing its gifts to the table, efforts can be intensified locally, nationally, and globally. Collaborations are an essential part of justice ministry—and historically, no entity has collaborated more effectively than has the African American church.

We have seen how the internal components of ministries of justice—care of the soul, education of congregation and community, political action and awareness, and collaborations—are all essential in serving those infected and affected by HIV/AIDS. Now let's look at some snapshot examples of other ministries that encompass both charity and justice.

Housing Ministry

Charity

- Helping people find housing
- Teaching people about credit
- Teaching about the benefits of owning as opposed to renting

Justice

- Fighting predatory lenders
- Fighting redlining of neighborhoods

Prison Ministry

Charity

- Visiting those who are in prison in person or in letter
- Sending care packages to those in prison

Justice

- Taking action against police brutality
- Taking action against disproportionate sentencing of blacks as opposed to whites in what is termed by attorney Michelle Alexander as "The New Jim Crow"

Health Ministry

Charity

- Providing resources for affordable or free health care
- Educating people with regard to various illnesses and maladies
- Educating people in ways to be well through eating, exercise, etc.

Justice

- Fighting for affordable health care access for all
- Fighting for affordable access to medications

Again, as we said in the introduction, these ministries are essential but not exhaustive.

External

In social justice work, many issues are overwhelming and therefore require key collaborations. While chapter 5 provides more details on how to identify external partners, here we discuss six benefits of establishing such partnerships: adequate resources, human capital, intellectual capital, visibility, credibility, and diversity.

First, access to *adequate resources* is often a challenge for those who seek to engage in systematic justice work. Partnering with external organizations and individuals is essential to sustainability. Second, solid partnership expands *human capital*. Expansion of people power becomes a significant factor. Remember the proverb "Together the ants ate the elephant." Responsibilities, duties, and tasks can be distributed according to skill sets and resources. Third, social justice work requires much reading and research. Partnering with think tanks, colleges and universities, specialists, and experts in given disciplines expands *intellectual capital.*

Drawing attention to an issue or a movement is a fourth pivotal step. The collaboration of organizations and individuals brings about more *visibility* of an issue, because each partner can promote the same cause to its respective audience. Additionally, in most cases the media is likely to cover events that take place among multiple groups, drawing more attention to a cause.

Fifth, external partnerships can build organizational *credibility*. For lesser-known churches or organizations, partnering with other trustworthy and respected groups can be beneficial. With that thought in mind, it is vital to be consistent and committed.

Finally, collaborating effectively demonstrates *diversity*. Few issues are based solely on race, class, religion, or ethnicity, although most of them comprise some combination of these issues. Even issues that have their largest impact on a specific demographic will benefit from having a broader base of universal advocacy. For example, when Christians and Jews rally behind their Muslim brothers and sisters to protest profiling based on race and religion, their witness is made more powerful. When whites and blacks join their Hispanic and Asian neighbors to lobby for a more hospitable immigration policy, their voices are amplified. When all residents in an area come together to fight for a failing public school district, change can be effected that impacts everyone in a community, city, and region. The race, religion, and ethnic background of students receiving a poor education are not the central issues. The level of resources invested in schools and communities where the poor, black, and brown live and the fate of the next generation are everyone's concern.

The crux of social justice work is confronting institutions that systematically create inequity and produce needs. Coming together across lines of race, religion, and ethnicity makes justice issues matters of human rights and not the exclusive problem of one marginalized minority.

Neighborhood Legal Clinic

Friendship-West Baptist Church in Dallas is committed to doing all it can to level the legal playing field for the citizens of its city who are economically challenged. The Dallas Volunteer Attorney Program (DVAP) exists to provide pro bono legal services to the underserved through the volunteer efforts of Dallas attorneys. In 2009 Friendship-West partnered with DVAP to make pro bono legal services available in a Dallas locale known as the Oak Cliff area, which has approximately 500,000 residents. Prior to establishing this partnership, there were no such services available in the area. With this partnership, however, on every third Wednesday individuals could come to the church and secure legal assistance and representation in a variety of civil matters. This has created a great opportunity for those who are in need of legal advice to speak directly with attorneys. The legal clinic is currently run by committed community volunteers, such as judges, paralegals, and attorneys, and members of the church's social action ministry.

Levels of Engagement

No one can look out on the typical urban landscape in this nation and not be moved by the distressed conditions of various communities. Personal knowledge, academic research, and case studies on the unhealthy conditions of local communities invite questions such as, "Who is responsible for rescuing the communities?" and "How can this be done?" People with hearts of compassion and commitment to advocacy for basic human rights and justice are faced with the task of engaging individuals. The primary foundation for engagement is relationships.

One way of addressing such questions lies in the ability of the church to recruit volunteers who can work together to establish relationships and collaborate. The extensive crises include, but are not limited to, overpriced goods in corner convenient stores, lack of access to quality grocery stores, dilapidated buildings, inferior public schools, vacant buildings, payday loan sharks, and auto title loans. These are all typical markers of exploitation in troubled communities.

Volunteers can partner to acquire personal knowledge, conduct academic research, and write case studies of such dastardly conditions. People with hearts of compassion and commitment to advocacy for basic human rights and justice can face this task together. The primary foundation for this engagement is relationships.

Volunteers are crucial for sustaining the work, but recruiting volunteers can be challenging. On one hand, people who have a genuine interest in the work may have other issues and options competing for their time and attention and therefore limited time and resources to devote to the work. On the other hand, it may be difficult to find volunteers who have both the right motives and the church's best interest at heart. Therefore, a vetting process through which passion and gifts are able to be discerned is critical to the success of the work. Chapter 4 deals with more details about this type of engagement. Levels of engagement can be identified in the following ways:

Individual

Dr. Haynes of Friendship-West Baptist Church in Dallas teaches a basic principle of leading and engaging individuals in justice work. He says, "You must show a person where she or he fits in the vision or the person will become a misfit." Essentially, Dr. Haynes is suggesting that we connect individuals to a vision of justice and/or a movement. This is accomplished through showing individuals how they personally fit and how they will benefit from being engaged.

To establish this fit, it is vital to know what resources, gifts, and talents individuals possess and how they can help advance the work. This is particularly important when recruiting for key leadership roles. Recruitment for leadership positions might be based on observations of people's leadership abilities that have become obvious through roles they have held in other areas of the local church. When Jesus recruited his disciples, he did not take out an ad in the daily newspaper; he took a personal approach. The disciples were recruited based on what Jesus knew about them personally. Jesus knew that the unique characteristics of each disciple would eventuate in the work being carried out once they merged.

In small churches where there are few volunteers, it is important to maximize the use of the talents of everyone involved. In larger churches, a net is often cast to gather laborers. Here the discernment process is crucial. It may be necessary to develop gifts inventories or to conduct well-designed discernment mechanisms to help people find which tasks they are best suited for. Likewise, it is also important to design ways that people can interact over time to form bonds and discover mutual strengths. Such bonds and relationships produce a sense of community and united fronts that are essential for attacking social justice issues together.

Congregational

Once individual volunteers are engaged, the next step is to connect them to others in the church family with whom they may have an affinity. Doing this will begin to expand the network of people who understand their part in the movement. In the larger group setting, the people can become engaged through messaging and action. For example, Sunday mornings are prime opportunities for leaders to speak to the masses through announcements. They have a captive audience, and therefore engagement is immediate. The announcements allow leaders to present the essentials of the issue briefly and to recruit people to participate in more extended educational meetings. It is also a time to move to action by distributing letters to be signed or inviting people to protests or demonstrations.

In Matthew 5, Jesus provides an example of this process in his Sermon on the Mount when he says, "Blessed are the poor in spirit. . . ." In this sermon he is both educating the disciples and calling them to action on behalf of the poor. When Jesus says someone is blessed, he is signifying that someone is worthy of honor. When Jesus describes the poor in spirit, he is speaking of those who are oppressed and exploited by the rich and powerful. Therefore he is instructing his disciples that those who are exploited by the empire are actually worthy of honor. Thus his followers must create an environment in which the downtrodden are honored and not exploited. Jesus is here communicating his position on the societal law and sermonically providing a series of lessons. Likewise, we must not only be prepared to speak and act on behalf of the poor, but we must also be prepared to advocate as well. In *True to Our Native Land*, Michael Brown defines the poor as "those for whom 'the system' does not work."[4] When Jesus says that the poor in spirit are to see the kingdom of God, that kingdom is in part the justice work the church does on their behalf. In addition to charity, it means dismantling the institutional evils that have resulted in their poverty.

Communal

As the internal family is connected, the church must move into the community. The community becomes engaged if it understands that the church is concerned about more than its own life. Therefore concerns about specific social justice issues must be communicated clearly. This means determining the most effective medium. Be it a community forum, television, the Internet, radio, or public cable, the message must be shared. The church must show itself to be the heartbeat of the community by staying in touch with the realities with which people deal between Sundays.

In the book of Esther, we find a model for engaging an entire community. The book says that Esther told Mordecai to go and tell all the Jewish people to fast for three days before she petitioned the king on their behalf. This collective action was a singular step that signified several things through one shared action: (1) identified committed members of the community, (2) demonstrated solidarity of that community, and (3) communicated common purposes/goals of that community. It was only after that groundwork was laid that the Jewish people were instructed to take action as a community in a unified way. The church must likewise first clearly demonstrate solidarity between the individuals and organizations who make up the community. Second, it must call for collective action. The Jews were aware that coming together for this collective action served a greater purpose beyond an individual. If the entire community did not stand together, it would suffer from the king's edict—detrimental public policy.

It should be noted that some justice issues do not have a specific ministry associated with them. Often these are issues that erupt over unpredictable community crises. Such issues may still need action from the church.

In such cases, organizations within the church can still form, using some of the components addressed above. As an example, in 2007 a major community uproar occurred over the Jena Six in Jena, Louisiana. In September, 2006, an African American student asked if they were allowed to sit under a tree at Jena High School. The student was told that they could sit wherever they wanted. The next day, from that same tree nooses were hung, seemingly in an attempt to warn other African Americans students from sitting under the same tree. High school officials discovered the three students responsible for the nooses and recommended expulsion. The superintendent overruled the expulsion and gave the three students responsible for the nooses a three-day suspension, stating that the nooses were a "youthful stunt." African American students protested such lenient treatment and organized a protest of such. On Monday, December 6, with racial tension still high, a white student who had been allegedly teasing and taunting an African American student regarding the nooses got into an altercation with some black students. The white student was taken to the hospital, released, and allegedly attended a social function the same evening. However, the black students were arrested and charged with attempted second-degree murder and expelled from school.

Many churches did not need to have a "Jena" ministry. Many churches and organizations simply committed to get involved and to act. Support was given for the victims' families through dollars and letters (care of the soul). Congregations were informed about the sequence of events (education), and prayer vigils were organized, buses were chartered, and letters were written to the judge and the district attorney of LaSalle Parish. Many organizations collaborated with each other to provide transportation, meeting space, access to phone hotlines, and other needed resources for organizing and mobilizing to right this wrong.

Another example is the case of Trayvon Martin, an unarmed black teen shot and killed by a town-watch member who claimed the violence was in self-defense. Again, many churches did not have a Trayvon Martin ministry, but many did organize to march in Sanford, Florida, and send letters to Sanford, and many collaborated in efforts to rally there. Moreover, the Trayvon Martin case has prompted many to look at clarifying or challenging legislation and policy, such as the Florida "Stand Your Ground" that would allow provide defense for such an act.

Ultimately, justice ministry occurred, using some if not all of the components discussed in this chapter.

We cannot say enough that the ministry of justice demands faithful people fighting for progress. Together we must eat the elephants of injustice that stampede our society and restore our planet!

NOTES

1. "Global HIV/AIDS estimates 2009, 2010" http://www.avert.org/world stats.htm.

2. HIV in the United States: At a Glance, http://www.cdc.gov/hiv/resources/factsheets/us.htm.

3. www.balmingilead.org.

4. Brian K. Blount, Cain Hope Felder, Clarice J. Martin, Emerson B. Powery, *True to Our Native Land* (Minneapolis: Fortress, 2007).

PART 2

Nuts & Bolts

CHAPTER 3
Laying the Foundations

In Genesis 6, God gave Noah specific instructions for how to construct the ark. Noah followed his instructions, and consequently the structure (inside and outside) was able to withstand the great flood. When developing social justice ministry, it is equally important to build an infrastructure that will withstand challenges and changes in leadership, socioeconomic demographics, and political realities over time. That is why the ministry/movement should never begin and end with a personality. Instead, its design should be based on a careful assessment of the community context in which it operates. Different types of justice work may call for different strategies.

This chapter provides practical guidelines paired with case studies that local church justice workers can use while building infrastructures within and outside the church. It provides case studies of structures that began within the walls of the church and extended into the community. It also provides studies of ministries and organizations that, with support from local churches, began outside the walls of the churches and extended into the community, both local and global. The case studies are accompanied by checklists and "things to keep in mind"—principles based on real-life experiences of practitioners from throughout the country. The chapter underscores the fact that the "laying of the bricks and mortar" must be guided by the context in which the work and walk of justice take place.

From Inside the Church

The foundational work within the church depends on the commitment of the leadership and on available resources. The authors have experience at churches that have built the ministry of justice into the fabric of the organization. An example is Trinity United Church of Christ in Chicago, where Rev. Reginald Williams Jr. served for six years (July 2002–August 2008). The pastor of Trinity at that time, Rev. Dr. Jeremiah A. Wright Jr., created a position titled associate pastor for justice ministries. The primary function was twofold: (1) to form partnerships with and between thirteen social justice ministries under one umbrella, and (2) to keep their respective ministry missions and work in concert with the mission and vision of the church.

It is important to underscore that the thirteen ministries involved worked together but in different areas of social justice. In their work both together and separately, they cared for souls and sought justice. For example, the health and wellness ministry educated church members about how to maintain healthy lifestyles while at the same time advocating at local, state, and national levels for eliminating unhealthy community conditions that caused unhealthy lifestyles. In other words, the mission of this ministry encompassed more than personal care and charity alone. Another branch of justice ministries, the prison ministry, cared for souls by visiting the incarcerated. It shared the gospel and kept in touch with inmates through letters. It also sponsored educational forums and advocated against abuses of the prison industrial complex. Such abuses included "stop and frisk," racial profiling, and mass incarceration. In other words, this ministry was organized not for charity purposes alone, but to eliminate the systemic ills of the prison system, a system that continues to grow at the expense of the vulnerable.

The above-mentioned ministries were created and sustained within a church that had the resources to sustain them. But how can a similar foundation be laid in a church that does not have such resources? The answer is found in the ministry, not the resources.

It is not the program but the principle behind the program that is important. One example is First Baptist Church of University Park, located in University Park, IL, the home of approximately 250 members. First Baptist Church does not have the amount of members, ministries, or money of other "mega" churches. However, it has made a commitment to the type of ministry that benefits the community. First Baptist Church of University Park has instituted a community awareness ministry whose mission is to bring community issues to the congregation's and community's awareness. Additionally this ministry is also charged with making the community aware of what the church offers to the community. While the church may not have "megachurch" resources, it does have people committed to "mega-ministry." Their activities have included letter-writing campaigns launched during worship services, candidates' forums held in the community, community forums which link elected officials and community members at times other than election time, and other educational forums which serve to apprise the congregation and community of important issues affecting the people of the community.

Using such methods, the church is addressing some social justice issues, such as the lack of grocery stores in the village and disparities in health care facilities. Furthermore, the church has been able to disseminate information about how to live healthy and whole lives. Education and activism do not require an abundance of resources. Building a social justice ministry within the local church requires people committed to do the work of justice. Small churches have conducted letter-writing campaigns, have partnered with other churches to change policies of local banks, and have challenged local representatives to sponsor legislation. All of these are examples of successful justice work being based on the stewardship of resources. While not every church can handle the same range of tasks, every church can handle some range of tasks. Regardless of context or resources, all can keep in mind Matthew 25:40, which says, "Just as you did it to one of the least of these who are members of my family, you did it to me."

Infrastructure

The first step in establishing a justice ministry is determining whether it should be classified as a nonprofit organization. As a nonprofit 501(c)3 organization, the church is positioned to extend ministry, impact communities, and increase the capacity of such ministries. Being classified as a nonprofit enables the church to receive grants from the government, various foundations, and individuals. More practical benefits will be discussed later in the chapter. If the church decides to create a justice ministry as a separate entity, decisions must be made as to its type of structure. The chart below provides a brief snapshot of options.

Nonprofit Corporations

NON-PROFIT STATUS	BENEFITS	REQUIREMENTS	DRAWBACKS
501(c)(3)	• It must be labeled as a charitable organization. • Contributions of individuals are tax deductible. • It is exempt from paying federal income taxes; state tax exemptions vary by state.	• It must not organize or operate for private interests. • It must not be organized or operate for the purpose of influencing legislation.	• It must not endorse, support, or campaign against a political candidate. • The amount of lobbying and political activity that it can do is restricted.
501(c)(4)	• It can participate in political campaigns as long as the activity is consistent with its purpose and is not the primary activity. • Lobbying is permitted.	• Organizations organize and operate exclusively to promote social welfare.	• Contributions to the organization are not tax deductible.

For additional information, visit: http://www.irs.gov/charities/churches/index.html.

To initiate the process of establishing a nonprofit 501(c)(3) or 501(c)(4) justice ministry, churches can seek out experienced people in the congregation (attorneys or persons with experience in the nonprofit world) or seek assistance from the local Center for Nonprofit Management organization. To take advantage of both worlds, churches can form both a 501(c)(3) and a 501(c)(4) organization. In the first case study below, you will find an organizational chart from Friendship-West Baptist Church that shows both types. All organizations listed in the following table are designated as 501(c)(3) organizations. The only exception is Citizens of Mizpah, which is designated as a 501(c)(4).

Case Study: Friendship-West Baptist Church Infrastructure

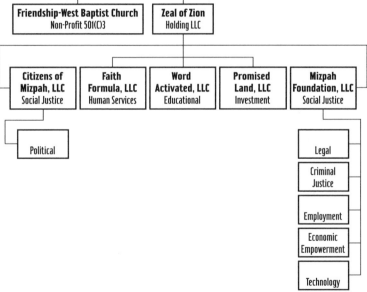

At Friendship, five nonprofit organizations were created to open funding and partnership opportunities. Faith Formula administers all service deliveries. Word Activated creates and implements all educational initiatives. Promised Land facilitates economic and planned development. Minister Danielle Ayers provides leadership to Mizpah Foundation and Citizens of Mizpah. Mizpah

Foundation offers programs and activities designed to address social issues and promote social activism. Citizens of Mizpah promotes advocacy and programs designed to strengthen the presence of citizens in the political process to achieve a more just society. Her position in both organizations provides insights into how these organizations can function in a local church.

Social justice activities are collectively carried out under the umbrella of Social Action Ministry. They are all designed to implement the church's mission statement: "The Friendship-West Baptist Church is called to be a caring community of Christians committed to developing a personal relationship with our Lord that eventuates into a ministry of evangelization, edification, and emancipation in the church and community." In keeping with this mission, the outline of the Social Action Ministry is as follows:

Mission

The mission of the Social Action Community is to strengthen the presence of people of color in the policy arena by combating destructive policy designs (unjust/unfair laws), policing regulatory guidelines, engaging in activism (direct action), and educating citizens on issues to promote human rights and democracy.

Impact Areas

Areas of impact which are essential to the church ministry and community-at-large are: economic empowerment, education, employment, legal, political action, environmental justice, and technology.

Strategies

The Social Action Community is committed to creating "communities of opportunities" by enlisting churches; community organizations; corporations; schools; city, state, and national government; and citizens to build stronger neighborhoods. Moreover, the Social Action Community will give a voice to marginalized peoples both nationally and internationally though purpose-driven activism to ensure full human rights.

The ministry is divided into six components. Volunteers currently provide leadership to each component. The following chart illustrates the components and reflects major areas of focus:

Part of establishing a successful and sustainable justice ministry is a clear purpose and statement of goals. For example, the Social Action Ministry has a mission statement for each component, containing a list of stated goals. The ministry mission statement tells the church and community why the Social Action Ministry exists. Each component has stated goals that drive ministry activity. It is essential for each to stay on task. The Economic Empowerment component, for example, has the following goals: (1) engage in and create opportunities for church and community to practice group economics, (2) educate and advocate for economic justice, (3) build up African American–owned businesses, (4) stimulate and increase economic activity in the southern sector, and (5) engage community corporations through monitoring social responsibility programs. Therefore any activity that takes place is focused on meeting one or more of these goals. Note that neither the ministry mission statement nor the goals supersedes the pastor's mission statement or the goals for the church. It is equally important to have a solid and well-documented orientation for new people who come into the ministry. Maintaining proper records is vital as well.

When new members join or express interest in the Social Action Ministry, they receive an email message welcoming them into the ministry with a notification of the time and location of the meeting. Upon arrival each new member receives a copy of the *Social Action Handbook*. This handbook communicates the goals of each component and includes a ministry roster. It also states the church and ministry mission and provides the vision statement. The ministry's strategies are also communicated as well. Each ministry meeting has a printed agenda to keep all minds on track and set the environment for a productive meeting.

Additionally, the ministry has established partnerships with various community actors in order to achieve the mission statement and to engage in justice work that is liberating for all. The right partnerships enable a church and community to acquire additional resources. Examples of such partnerships have included the Samuel DeWitt Proctor Conference, Prairie View A&M and Texas A&M Universities' extension programs, the Dallas League of Women Voters, and the Dallas Independent School District.

When forging such partnerships, there are a few things to keep in mind. First, it is important to be sure that the organization's and/or individual's agenda is consistent with that of the church. Second, it is vital to be sure that the organization and/or individual is credible. Research their profile and gain knowledge of their track record. Third, clearly defining roles, delineating responsibilities, and specifying the procedures for accountability within the partnerships is crucial. This can be done via a memorandum of understanding (MOU).

Things to Keep in Mind

1. Create and disseminate all organizational protocol to volunteers and staff. For example, Friendship-West has a booklet on policies and procedures for submitting requests for buildings and grounds (room assignments), audio visual equipment (microphones), and communications (bulletins, graphics).
2. Clearly communicate the organizational and reporting structures.
3. Provide a contact list of key staff.
4. Create a vehicle for systematically documenting all activities. It is important to chronicle the history of the church or organization. Proper documentation will be beneficial and key to securing funding from governmental agencies and/or foundations. Additionally, documentation demonstrates the organization's capacity to facilitate programs and activities. Documentation is also important to capture the history of the organization.

Organization of 501(c)(3)

Laying the Foundations

In the interview below, I (Min. Ayers) spoke with my ministerial colleague Rev. Rickey D. Hill about his unique perspective on how to develop the proper infrastructure from both a small church and megachurch context based on his experience at Friendship-West.

Ayers: What is your official role and title at Friendship-West Baptist Church?

Hill: I serve as the executive pastor and project director of Life Matters. (Life Matters is a program designed to educate and provide resources for healthy marriages in low-income African American communities.)

Ayers: Friendship-West has not always been a megachurch. Tell us a little bit about the evolution of the membership.

Hill: When I arrived at Friendship-West, the membership stood at approximately 75 to 150 or less. Through the years, the membership has grown to approximately 15,000. Sunday attendance averages around 7,000 to 9,000.

Ayers: Wow! So, with such church growth—moving from small church to megachurch—how has the infrastructure changed?

Hill: We started off operating as a nonprofit with limited human and financial resources. So we centered people around a cause in an effort to carry out ministry. We then evolved into a 501(c)(3) through exposure to business models. We did not know the benefits of obtaining a 501(c)(3) status in the early years. Additionally, over the years we created various staff-driven departments to carry out the ministry of the church.

Ayers: Would you recommend all churches to operate under a 501(c)(3) status regardless of size?

Hill: Yes. This move to use business techniques to build an infrastructure lays a solid foundation for spiritual and relational development in a small church. It also puts the church in a position to grow with systems already in place.

Ayers: What are some other benefits of operating as a 501(c)(3)?

Hill: There are several benefits. One, it allows leadership to make sound decisions not based on emotions. You have the governance of the

47

church in writing. Additionally, organizing as a 501(c)(3) clears the path for the church to seek funding it otherwise would not be able to qualify for as a nonprofit. Moreover, the government can't discriminate against the church.

Ayers: How has Friendship-West benefited from this organizational structure?

Hill: We have benefited in many ways from this structure. The most recent benefit was the receipt of a $500,000 grant for Life Matters. This federal funding enabled us to further expand the work beyond the walls of the church. We are able to perform tasks and access resources we did not have prior to the grant reward.

Ayers: Do you recommend that churches create additional 501(c)(3) organizations?

Hill: Absolutely. The development of additional 501(c)(3) organizations based on a specific purpose and initiative opens up opportunities. Collaborations become critical. For example, when we were a small church, we wanted to expand our HIV/AIDS ministry into the community to assist more people. We created FW (Friendship-West) Empowerment. Through this structure we partnered with various community organizations and government agencies. Additionally, we have established five more LLCs (Mizpah Foundation, Citizens of Mizpah, Word Activated, Promised Land, and Faith Formula Human Services) to carry out specific ministry activities.

Ayers: Does Friendship-West have any other initiatives under the LLCs you have established?

Hill: Yes. Faith Formula Human Services Corporation currently operates under three grants—Life Matters, Texans Credit Union, and Learn and Earn. The partners for Learn and Earn are United Way, City Square (formally known as Central Dallas Ministries), Volunteer Center of North Texas, Head Start of Greater Dallas, Dallas Housing Authority, Diabetes Health and Wellness Institute at Baylor, YWCA, and Chase Bank. The Learn and Earn program is also funded by community organizations. The Life Matters program is a federally funded grant.

Ayers: Are you aware of any additional resources that will assist the reader in learning more about organizing ministry?

Hill: Yes. I would recommend *Managing the Nonprofit Organization: Principles and Practices* by Peter F. Drucker.

Rev. Hill lays out a compelling argument for churches to operate under a 501(c)(3). Organizations are in a better position to apply for and receive funding. Collaborations become essential for successful ministry. Additionally, churches can take advantage of a business model that outlines the governance of the church in writing.

From Outside the Church

From outside of the physical walls of the church, many have explored doing the work of the church through various means. Ministries of justice are set up and organized from outside the church but still do the work of the church based on the organizations' sense of a call to the ministry of justice.

Case Study: Romal Tune, Clergy Strategic Alliances and Faith Leaders for Change

Rev. Romal Tune, based in Washington, DC, is the founder of Clergy Strategic Alliances and Faith Leaders for Change and is a consultant to churches and nonprofits on issues of empowerment and justice. His most recent venture is Faith Leaders for Change, which focuses on justice in education. Back in 2005 he created Clergy Strategic Alliances in response to the devastation of Hurricane Katrina. Various organizations requested Rev. Tune's assistance in bringing together religious leaders from across the country to provide aid to those adversely affected by Hurricane Katrina in southern Louisiana, the Gulf Coast, and parts of Mississippi. First he brought faith leaders together both to visit New Orleans and to commit financial and human resources. Then he sensed God's call to strategically partner with people across religious and political lines to focus on needs for justice. In describing the inception of the organization, he says, "Clergy Strategic Alliances was created to strategically bring together leaders from different sectors who have common interests and for the benefit of adding value to the work of nonreligious and religious organizations in ways that help people."[1]

Currently, Clergy Strategic Alliances is a consultant-based entity. Rev. Tune explains, "We work on behalf of clients seeking to build relationships with the religious community on a specific issue, such as poverty, education, health care, etc. This structure allows us to identify clients that are a good fit for communities of faith seeking to help people in need. It allows us to help communities of faith identify good partners, and it also allows us to research organizations and companies that might be a good fit for partnerships with people of faith based on what their company is doing."[2]

Rev. Tune's latest venture, Faith Leaders for Change, has evolved out of his work with many of his clients who deal with the specific issue of education. He has exposure to many communities around the country who are in dire straits and find themselves addressing a myriad of issues related to public education. It should be noted here that many of the issues related to public education are also directly related to the prison industrial complex. In many of these schools, children are, in no uncertain terms, essentially being prepared for prison. Prisons that are traded on Wall Street also have subsidiary companies that specialize in educational testing. So with the scores of failing schools, those in power are predicting how many privatized prisons to build. Taken further, one can note that the efforts of mass incarceration are targeting black and brown children at a disproportionate and immoral level. Therefore justice in education is an important issue not only for Rev. Tune but for the entire community.

To address the education crisis, Rev. Tune has organized Faith Leaders for Change specifically to work with churches for the purpose of improving student performance while simultaneously working with "at-risk" youth to equip them with necessary tools for living. Rev. Tune's advice to those organizing ministries of justice is this:

> Build strategic partners locally and nationally. You can do far more
> for your community working with allies than you will ever do on

your own. Building infrastructures is critical to the longevity and sustainability of the work. Make sure that whatever you do can be measured or quantified. Be sure that goals are set, and that deliverables are clear. It is important to be able to show that what you are doing is making a difference so that you can have a clear way of attributing success to the work you are doing. Success should be based on evidence that what you are doing is working, not on feeling good about it alone. If you can prove that it works and you are making a difference, then that will motivate people to feel good about it and continue doing it.[3]

Case Study: Iva E. Caruthers, General Secretary, Samuel DeWitt Proctor Conference

Dr. Iva E. Caruthers is general secretary of the Samuel DeWitt Proctor Conference, a network of people of faith who collectively share the burden to do the work of justice. She explains, "The Samuel DeWitt Proctor Conference, Inc. (SDPC) represents a cross section of progressive African American faith leaders and their congregations in the United States. Founded in 2003 as a 501(c)(3) organization, the SDPC was called into being to continue the rich legacy of the faith community's engagement in issues of social justice."[4]

> The mission of the Samuel DeWitt Proctor Conference (SDPC) is to nurture, sustain, and mobilize the African American faith community in collaboration with civic, corporate, and philanthropic leaders to address critical needs of human and social justice within local, national, and global communities. SDPC seeks to strengthen the individual and collective capacity of thought leaders and activists in the church, academy, and community through education, advocacy, and activism. Through partnerships and collaborations with others from the academic, business, policy, and not-for-profit communities, the skills, talents, and resources of SDPC supporters are maximized by sharing information and models of successful outreach strategies.[5]

One project of the annual SDPC is the annual conference, which serves as a think tank of leaders from throughout the country regarding specific crises facing African American communities. In February 2011, the conference focused on mass incarcerations of black men and women in response to Michelle Alexander's book *The New Jim Crow*. At that conference, an action plan was launched. During the following year, regional conferences were held to brainstorm and plan. One of the outcomes was a website and a study guide to accompany the use of the book in local churches throughout the country. The website also offers other publications dealing with similar issues and a blog whereby national and international leaders can brainstorm over issues facing the community at large.

The SDPC international newsletter alerts church and non-church members of issues of concern to the black community at large, such as issues surrounding the murder of Trayvon Martin. Through the website, clergy and laity participate in letter-writing campaigns. SDPC, partnering with seminaries throughout the country to bring a new generation of faith leaders to the annual conference, offers seminary credit and opportunities to brainstorm with other seminarians and various faith leaders about issues of critical concern. Such forums always deal with the topic of how faith communities can respond to crises of justice both domestically and internationally.

Case Study: The Earthquake in Haiti and a Partnership for Global Mission

Connecting the global dots is another aspect of creating a solid foundation for social justice. While building and engaging, churches must explore natural linkages with social justice issues throughout the world. Brothers and sisters across the globe are connected. Recently, brothers and sisters in Egypt, Tunisia, and South Sudan, in their own ways, participated in their own respective fights for freedom. Many of the movements have been energized by African American movements for freedom, equality, and justice. The widespread civil disobedience was prompted by dictatorships, human rights violations, government corruption, and extreme poverty. The prophet Amos makes a plea for global justice on behalf of the oppressed. In chapters 1 and 2, he calls for a movement that requires facing oppressive institutional actions.

The importance of seeking global justice is underscored by the fact that people from throughout the world are dependent on each other for essential goods and services. There are very few consumer products that do not pass through various countries before finally reaching those who will consume them. For example, in the aftereffects of the devastating tsunami in Japan, a General Motors plant in the United States had to be shut down due to lack of parts from Japan, directly impacting the American labor force. Now more than ever countries around the globe are dependent on one another. Therefore people must be concerned about what goes on in their neighborhood, cities, states, country, and global communities.

No more visible has been this interconnectedness than in the history of Haiti. Haitians had never given up the battle of its ancestors that began more than two hundred years ago when they initiated the first and only successful slave revolution and created the first independent black republic in the world. In fact, their ability to break free from colonizers gave rise to revolutions in the global South. Throughout Southern communities, resistance came in the forms of organized women, peasants, clergy, laity, workers, and others. Their mobilizations, protests, and advocacy have brought down dictators, staved off some of the worst economic policies, and kept themselves from going quietly into obscurity as defeated people.

However, on January 12, 2010, the island of Hispaniola experienced a devastating earthquake. What the earthquake ultimately revealed was the man-made disaster that had plagued Haiti for years—the degenerative foreign policy of America, France, and other nations. Dr. Haynes visited the country in July of 2010. Following Dr. Haynes's visit, Minister Ayers traveled to Haiti along with Rev. Rick Hill and Tyra Clemons (Friendship-West Staff), a native of Haiti, and others. The trip was life-changing. Upon returning, Haynes, Hill, Clemons, and Ayers met to develop a mission model for engaging Haiti. To begin this process, Friendship-West connected with Dr. Iva Carruthers of the Samuel DeWitt Proctor Conference and Dr. David Goately of the Lott

Carey Mission. Lott Carey is a 114-year-old foreign mission organization that specializes in Christian mission around the world. The group (Friendship-West, Samuel DeWitt Proctor, and Lott Carey) is currently in the process of collectively developing long- and short-term strategies to mobilize resources and organize the work locally, nationally, and internationally to address restoration and foreign policy issues. They are hopeful that this impromptu partnership will allow them to join the Haitians in "setting the captives free."

In this chapter, we have presented some guidelines and case studies for laying the foundations for social justice ministry. We have offered examples of beginning within the physical walls of the church and extending out into the community and of initiating the work outside of the community with partnerships between local, national, and global leaders.

Nelson Mandela helps bring this notion of laying the foundation home for us. Dennis A. Jacobsen, in his book *Doing Justice: Congregations and Community Organizing*, begins chapter 10 by reflecting on Mandela's amazing autobiography. Mandela is quoted as saying, "The freedom struggle is not merely a question of making speeches, holding meetings, passing resolutions, and sending deputations, but of meticulous organization, militant mass action, and above all the willingness to suffer and sacrifice."[6] Jacobsen further reflects that "meticulous organization requires ongoing discipline. . . . The mission of the church cannot be carried out in any sustained fashion without structure, trained leaders, a network of relationships, and substantial money."[7] The organization of ministries of justice requires that actions that come from the organization sufficiently serve the cause of justice. Nowhere is the need for meticulous organization more apparent than when the church engages in the work of community organization, the topic of the next chapter.

////////

NOTES

1. Rev. Romal Tune, Personal Interview, November 13, 2011.
2. Ibid.
3. Ibid.
4. Dr. Iva Caruthers, Personal Interview, November 13, 2011.
5. See http://www.sdpconference.info/index.php?option=com_k2&view
=itemlist&layout=category&task=category&id=11&Itemid=294, accessed
November 19, 2012.
6. Dennis A. Jacobsen, *Doing Justice: Congregations and Community
Organizing* (Minneapolis: Fortress, 2001), 79.
7. Ibid.

CHAPTER 4

Pursuing Things
Hoped For

///

*Now faith is the substance of things hoped for, the evidence of
things not seen.*

—Hebrews 11:1 KJV

The focus of this chapter is to inspire the reader to pursue permanent change in social structures that currently perpetuate injustice. We begin with basic foundational principles for engaging in social justice work as it relates to community development and organizing. Community development can be defined as a process of taking a community assessment, leveraging community assets, connecting with outside resources to fill "structural holes," and engaging in advocacy that leads to permanent change.

We will utilize a general typology to understand community development according to economists Ronald F. Ferguson and William T. Dickens. Ferguson and Dickens have identified five major components in the community development process. They use the language of "capital" to describe the variety of resources needed to effect change and build community.

Key Community Elements

Physical Capital	Buildings, tools, real estate, etc.
Intellectual and Human Capital	Skills, knowledge, and confidence
Social Capital	Norms, shared understandings, trust, professional and social networks
Financial Capital	Money, "Benjamins," greenbacks
Political Capital	Combining and leveraging the above types of capital to influence political outcomes as well as to gain access to the political structures (local, county, state, national)

Source: Adapted from F. Ronald Ferguson and T. William Dickens, *Urban Problems and Community Development* (Washington, DC: Brookings Institute, 1999), 4–5.

In the context of the biblical foundation, this typology will provide a base for further exploration on how to engage in social justice work. This chapter is about community organizing from a faith perspective. When thinking about such organizing and "things hoped for," the biblical figure of Nehemiah comes to mind—a man who proved to have great integrity, faith, and commitment to community. He was among the more fortunate Jewish exiles. Although far removed from his own people, Nehemiah lived a comfortable life in a distant country, working in a senior-level government post. Then he got word that his community was suffering from lack of development and protection. He felt compelled to return home and engage in community development, repair social and religious networks, serve in politics, and organize by faith, hoping for restorative justice. As a consequence, a collective effort took place among community stakeholders and residents, and the walls were restored. Many have met this man in the pages of the sacred text that bears his name. Nehemiah demonstrates what it means to fully engage in community development and organization from a position of faith.

Is this not the testimony of those who are called to be a voice on behalf of those who live on the margins of society by confronting injustices? This work, at times, can be lonely and liberating, both a blessing and a burden. Those who are committed must move forward with events, activities, and programs that will bring about liberation for the people and communities being served. But regardless of the wide variety of outcomes, it is necessary to commit to the call to make a difference in the world by changing the systems and institutions that preclude those being served from living an abundant life. In many instances, one must operate from a disposition of things hoped for. Proper tools are necessary for beginning the work.

There is a powerful symbol to be found in Nehemiah's narrative. When Nehemiah heard about the plight of the Jewish remnant that remained behind in Jerusalem and the surrounding region, he wanted to help. He wanted to rebuild the ruins of his people—and in a time and place where safety was found within the walls of a city, the priority task became rebuilding the walls of the Holy City, Jerusalem. Nehemiah began with tapping into his political capital. The text says Nehemiah asked the king for permission to rebuild Jerusalem (Nehemiah 2:5).

The work of social justice is, in a real way, a ministry of rebuilding—of repairing the cracked and tumbled-down structures of society that have created vulnerability for its citizens. And so, while acknowledging the pragmatic necessity of Ferguson and Dickens's capital, we will refer to the foundational principles as "walls," the structures that frame a stable and secure society with just systems and righteous boundaries. Only within such walls might a community become fully functioning with safe space to live and serve all of God's people.

Inspecting the Wall (Community Asset Map)

The first thing Nehemiah did upon his return to Jerusalem was to inspect the walls of the city to determine their condition and develop an action plan. The motivation for inspecting a given wall may come in the form of one or more social justice issues demanding attention. With that in mind, the first step is to assess the specific nature of the situation. For Nehemiah the inspection of the walls was the first step toward rebuilding the temple, which was the symbol of God's presence with the Jewish people. But it was impossible to consider a major reconstruction of the fallen temple without strong walls, which created a protected space in which to work.

In biblical times, walls served as protection for a city, and the quality of the walls indicated the health of the community. Comparably, the walls of a modern community are the infrastructures that nurture quality of life there. One must take time to think, study, and assess where the community is and then develop an action plan. When inspecting or assessing a community, it is important to focus on what it has more than on what it does not have. Communities might have more social, intellectual, physical, and financial capital than seems readily apparent.

Asset mapping is the process of determining what assets the community possesses. This process uncovers the strengths and weaknesses of a community's walls (social, intellectual, physical, financial, and political capital). Assessment can begin with brainstorming what is in the community. For example, you may do Internet research to determine how many postsecondary institutions (intellectual capital) are in the community. Or you may use Nehemiah's model of visually inspecting the structures in the community (physical capital).

The following is an example of a community asset map (acquired after an inspection of the "walls"). Gangs are a form of social capital. Some consider it a negative form of social capital. They must be considered in the community landscape as people organize for change in their communities.

The community of faith is placed in the center to represent the starting point. An initial internal assessment should be conducted before looking externally. After taking an assessment of the community, the next goal is to gain a more in-depth understanding of the political landscape.

Answering the following questions is important:

Political Landscape

Who Is Representing the Community?

LOCAL MUNICIPALITY AND COUNTY

1. Who are the elected officials at each level?

2. Who represents your district? Consider the residences of church leaders and parishioners and the church building.

3. What are their core issues?

4. Are these core issues consistent with the church and the community's core issues?

5. What is the background of the local officials?

6. What is the track record of local officials on making positive substantive changes? Have they improved the quality of life for their constituents?

7. How often do the local officials interact with the community? Do they host town hall meetings? Do they keep the community abreast of changes "downtown" that will affect the community before they happen?

8. Do local officials stay in contact with the community beyond election day?

STATE AND NATIONAL

(Repeat survey questions 1–8)

9. Do local officials serve on any committees? What are these committees? What are their positions on such committees?

10. What is the track record of local officials on introducing and/or voting on legislation that impacts the community being served by the church? Are these issues of importance to the social justice ministry of the church? Are they important for the well-being of the community?

This is not an exhaustive survey. Expand the list of survey questions as seems suited to your community. Note that addressing a given issue will move the investigation beyond the people who represent the church community to key representatives who may need to be contacted about other issues.

Social Networks (Connectors)

Who Is Out There? Who Is Known? Who Is Not Known?

Take an inventory of individuals (decision makers) who are located in the immediate community and beyond. Not all "need to know" people exist in one place. Create a list of their names and other critical information.

1. Which individuals are already known by people involved in the church's social justice ministry?

2. Which influencers are you least familiar with?

3. Who are leaders in name only? This assessment will take a degree of skill. Know where they fit and place them accordingly.

Community and Congregational Profile

Community

1. What is the ethnic makeup of the city and of the immediate community surrounding the church? (Resources: census.gov, city hall records, reports produced by local research institutes)

2. What is the economic profile of the city? (Resources: city's economic development office and local research institutes)

3. What is the ethnic makeup of the public schools by district? What is the economic profile of the public schools by district? (Resources: school district administrative offices)

4. What is the main source of the city's economy (textiles, agriculture, manufacturing, etc.)?

5. How many households are in the community? How many are headed by single parents? How many are headed by grandparents?

6. How many quality grocery stores (fresh produce, a variety of products, name-brand products, products that have not exceeded the expiration date, clean aisles, good customer service, etc.) are in the community?

7. Where are the main retail centers? What type of products do they offer?

8. What is the number of registered voters?

   Republican _____ Democrat _____ Independent _____
   (Resource: County election department)

9. What is the history of the city? (e.g., founders, date, significant events, political history, population and economic development trends, historic events, economic hardships,

hometown heroes, family legacies, far-reaching individual tragedies or victories, etc.)

Congregation

1. Where do the members live? Do most live in the vicinity of the church? If not, in what areas do they reside?

2. What are the gifts and talents of the parishioners? Take an inventory of the various professional competencies or vocational interests in the church.

3. What is the economic breakdown of the membership? (This can be gathered anonymously and can serve as an indicator of financial potential.)

4. How many small business owners exist in the church? Develop a list of minority-owned businesses.

DEMOGRAPHICS

5. What are the ages? 0–12 ____ 13–18 ____ 19–35 ____
   36–55 ____ 56 and up ____

6. What are the number of households?

7. How many households are headed by single mothers?

8. How many households are headed by single fathers?

9. How many households are headed by grandparents?

ETHNIC MAKEUP OR COUNTRY OF ORIGIN

African American ____ Caucasian ____ Hispanic ____ Asian____
Arab____ Haitian ____ Dominican ____ Nigerian ____
Ethiopian ____ Other _____ Other _____
Other _____ Other _____

Over the years, we have picked up many insightful ways of being reflective within the context of serving in ministry. The following questions emerged out of several conversations with the brilliant and experienced international justice fighter Dr. David

E. Goatley, executive secretary-treasurer of Lott Carey Foreign Mission Convention. Answering the following set of questions will provide a solid foundation for building and sustaining a substantive justice ministry. Insert the name of the faith community or organization in the appropriate blank.

1. The core values of _____ are:

   • _____

   • _____

   • _____

2. How long has _____ been in the community?

3. What does _____ do best?

4. Where does _____ do its best work?

5. Where do you want to focus the passions of _____?

6. When addressing issues, what is _____'s commitment (time frame)? How will resources be allocated? Who will be responsible for strategy and operational procedures? Where will the power to make decisions reside?

7. How is _____ perceived in the community and the city? When people hear the name _____, what do they think?

Taking the Issue to the People

Upon completing the typology for community development, the next step is placing the issue(s) before the people. After Nehemiah surveyed the walls, he had an idea of the strength and weaknesses of the community. He formed a development plan and then communicated the state of the community to the people. At this point in the process, it is important to communicate key community issues in a systematic manner. This requires organizing. Organizing can be defined as persuading individuals to commit to a given cause or organization by arranging and communicating issues in a systematic manner. Pastoral support in the local church and executive-level support in community organizations is an important factor at this point and for future organizing. Those charged with organizing will need appropriate leadership to communicate and publicly demonstrate that they are behind the messages that are sent throughout the church and into the community. This is crucial, because after completing the "wall" inspection, it is of critical importance to expose the issues to the congregation and community at large. The information must be communicated in a manner that enables all to understand and connect. Dramatization and education are two options.

Dramatization can be used to show the effects of the element(s) creating the injustice. Various forms of social media (podcasts, Facebook, blogs, YouTube, apps, Internet forums, etc.), documentaries, and television can be critical assets in telling the story and gaining support.

> Example: Using television, civil rights leaders successfully portrayed human suffering at the hands of a southern oppressive structure brought on by Jim Crow policies.

Educating oneself, parishioners, and the public at large provides a solid foundation. This can be done in the form of fact sheets, voter guides, bulletin inserts, and other accessible forms of media. Having pastoral support that will enable education to take place as part of the sermon and/or the worship service is helpful.

> Example: A set amount of time can be allocated to educate parishioners on an issue during a worship service. The time should be limited and the message concise and to the point. In a recent justice initiative at Friendship-West, time was set aside time during the worship service to update the congregation on what had taken place related to a given justice effort. Additionally, opportunities for action were offered.

Equally important is what we communicate in an effort to maintain support of the people. Communication of outcomes provides vision and direction. Clearly communicate the desired outcome(s) of a justice initiative to parishioners, citizens, and supporters.

Example: In the southern sector of Dallas, an adult entertainment business was set to open within walking distance of an elementary school located in a residential community. The following desired outcomes were clearly communicated to supporters, elected officials, citizens, and parishioners: (1) Revisit zoning and make the necessary changes to prevent primary educational facilities from being included within the same zoning ordinances as adult entertainment businesses. (2) Bring construction to an immediate standstill. (3) Locate an alternative business or public use for the facility. (4) Introduce legislation at the state level that would make it unprofitable for adult entertainment businesses to operate in local communities.

Communicating progress is imperative to keep parishioners, supporters, and citizens updated on any progress—or lack of progress. In cases where there may not be any movement or change on the issue, communicate why the stagnation has occurred, and explain about any roadblocks or opposition. Use community forums, email blasts, Sunday morning worship services, fact sheets, and postings on blogs, Facebook, or other social media. A combination of media formats may be necessary.

To bring more clarity for engaging in a particular action or justice initiative, communicating the consequences of inaction and the benefits of taking action is indispensable. List the possible negatives and positives that will be manifested if the injustice is not corrected. Make sure you have thoroughly researched the issue(s), and communicate in a straightforward fashion.

Example: In Texas, the Texas State Board of Education has the power to determine curriculum. Some state board representatives with no educational background rewrote the history curriculum in textbooks. The approval of the new curriculum took place during a state board meeting with little to no debate or input from academic experts. An immediate grassroots movement consisting of Friendship-West, community organizations, and elected officials took place to remove the board's power to determine curriculum. Literature was distributed in the churches and community to clearly educate the public on the consequences of inaction and the benefits of action to remove this power from the State Board of Education.

Employing the People

Nehemiah took a community assessment, communicated the condition of the community to the people, and then employed people power. When we reach the third chapter of Nehemiah, we see the people at work. The typology here can assist us with engaging in community development and developing justice initiatives. The next strategic step is mobilizing, drawing individuals together for the purpose of taking action. Pastoral support in the local church and executive-level support in community organizations are critical at this mobilization point. Individuals respond more readily if they see top leadership engaged in "feet to the ground" activities.

Community meetings are a way of pulling a large number of supporters together to move into action. Central to mobilizing is the education of supporters on the issues. Concluding meetings with an action item to get citizens involved facilitates a degree of ownership and provides an opportunity for them to be a part of the solution. City council meetings are useful in pulling supporters together for the purpose of exercising their voices in a democracy. Attendance also helps to keep elected officials honest.

Example: A community meeting was held to address the dastardly actions of the Texas State Board of Education mentioned above. At the conclusion of the meeting, supporters had the opportunity to write the Education Committee chair, Senator Florence Shapiro, and ask that she take immediate and necessary steps to remove the power of the State Board to determine curriculum.

Example: On a quarterly basis, First Baptist Church of University Park's Community Awareness Ministry sponsors a community forum in which residents from University Park, Illinois, and other area suburbs can come to raise issues and map out ways to address issues. All are welcome, including elected officials. This allows for education about competing perspectives and for confrontation if necessary.

Marches, group advocacy, and rallies can reflect the public support that is behind an issue. They can also be utilized to symbolically demonstrate displeasure about a public policy or systemic injustice.

Example: Advocacy Days at the state capitol. Engaging citizens in the process of advocating at the state level provides an opportunity for them to speak directly to elected officials who are in a position to change or construct public policy. Moreover, this experience causes citizens to take ownership of the issues and make them personal. They carry the message and speak for themselves and/or on behalf of a given beneficiary group. Friendship-West collaborated with Representative Helen Giddings, local hospitals, child advocates, and other community organizations to push for public policy changes in the Children's Health Insurance Plan (CHIP). Parishioners were educated on proposed policy changes to correct the administrative policies that precluded millions of children from receiving health care coverage. An opportunity was made available for citizens to write letters, make phone calls, and speak to legislators/staffers on behalf of children in the state of Texas.

Building people power through civic engagement activities is an invaluable tool. For the purpose of this book, *civic engagement* refers to initiatives that seek to empower the church and community in the political and electoral process. In recent elections, voter fraud, intimidation, and suppression in the public square and at the polls attempted to produce voter apathy in many communities of color. However, as evidenced in the most recent Presidential election of 2012, these efforts were overcome as the Obama campaign was able to garner a coalition from various constituencies which overcame the efforts and attempts to disenfranchise and compromise the people's vote.

There are several methods of empowering through education that can be implemented to overcome such negative efforts aimed at voter disenfranchisement.

1. Publishing and distributing voter's rights guides is a vital way to get information into the hands of potential voters. Information on voter's rights can be obtained through county election departments, the local League of Women's Voters, and other civic groups.

2. Voter education guides (based on candidate questionnaires) empower and equip people. Potential candidates must be held accountable by answering critical and relevant questions that directly provide insight about how they plan to serve their communities. This can be done by selecting a small group to develop a questionnaire to be submitted to all candidates (Republican, Democrats, Independents, etc.). The results should be published and distributed (hard copy, email, downloaded from a website, etc.) to the church and community.

3. Political forums serve as spaces to connect candidates and citizens. Those vying for elected offices are given the opportunity to share the policies they will implement should they be elected. And voters are given the opportunity to investigate the candidates so that they can cast educated votes.

4. Voter registration and turnout programs are pivotal steps in the civic engagement process. A core foundation of United States democracy is a citizen's right to vote. Voter registration and turnout can serve as political equalizers and promote inclusiveness. Citizens are empowered to vote for candidates who represent their interests. As a consequence, we must have solid programs that promote ongoing participation in the electoral process.

Civic Engagement Education Forums
Meet the Candidates Forum at Friendship-West Baptist Church

The focus was on two major issues central to Dallas County in 2010: the criminal justice system and the county budget. The 2010 forum focused on the races for county judge and district attorney. Friendship collaborated with the League of Women Voters to produce a comprehensive voter's guide to educate voters. Approximately three hundred community residents attended the forum, including three local media channels [4 (FOX News), 8 (ABC), and 11 (CBS)] and other elected officials. Additionally, the church utilized U-Stream to enable citizens to view the forum and chat via the Web. Countless volunteers came together to welcome Dallas citizens from various neighborhoods and to serve as timekeepers, moderators, and contacts for the press and for the candidates.

Candidates Forum at First Baptist Church of University Park

In April of 2011, the village of University Park, Illinois, selected a new mayor and new trustees. Prior to this election, First Baptist Church of University Park hosted a candidates' forum where voters were able to ask the candidates questions. The forums took place over two days, Sunday and Tuesday. Approximately seventy-five people attended each evening and were able to be educated before early voting began.

Notice that the same type of forum took place in two different contexts. Friendship-West is a large congregation in a metropolitan city, Dallas, and First Baptist Church of University Park is a smaller congregation in a suburb of Chicago, University Park. We mention this to further underscore our admonition to do what you can right where you are in whatever context you find yourself.

Community Forum at First Baptist Church of University Park

The Community Awareness Ministry has committed to hosting community forums in University Park on a quarterly basis. The aim of the community forums is to bring together elected officials and the citizenry, at a time other than election time, in order to allow for the raising and addressing of issues important to the community. This effort allows for a few important elements to occur. Primarily it connects the citizens with elected officials more than once every election cycle. More importantly, it allows the elected officials to be held accountable to their constituency during their terms of office.

Advocacy is another way to mobilize people for movement building. The term *advocacy* translates into political involvement. The term *politics* often causes clergy, lay leaders, and even some community organizers to shy away from engaging in any activity that might be perceived as confrontational or that might draw attention to their church or organization. The reality is that politics informs every aspect of life. Political involvement includes registering to vote, voting in elections, and protesting. In matters of social justice, however, political involvement must go beyond these activities. Engaging in public policy is central to advocacy efforts, for public policy is a vehicle for carrying out government decisions about how and to whom societal resources are to be distributed.

Those who efficiently build and maintain "walls" will be better equipped to make permanent changes. Maintaining the walls, however, is not an easy task and it requires both faith and deeds. In his essay "From Vision to Action," Dr. Haynes says, "The church must not limit its ministry to feeding fish to the poor or even teaching them how to fish, but the church needs to ensure that the lake is free of contaminants and then empower the disadvantaged to buy the lake."[1] He calls for the progression of moving beyond social services to community development and onward to justice. Justice calls for moving beyond individual impact and temporary relief to group impact and permanent relief. That is, "the church needs to ensure that the lake is free of contaminants and then empower the disadvantaged to buy the lake."

This suggests that one must research to educate oneself about an issue in order to determine who or what precludes the south side of town from flourishing, for example. Then one can more effectively engage in necessary activities. It is important to leverage the "walls" to change current policies or implement new policies to make sure the lake is never contaminated again. The end goal of social justice work is to change the system and thereby have a positive and permanent impact on those who are socially disadvantaged.

Points to Remember When Advocating

Do:

- Make an appointment with elected officials, committee chairs, and/or staffers.
- Establish and follow legislative priorities.
- Dress neatly, comfortably, and for the occasion.
- Get an early start to avoid anything that might delay the route to the appointment. Be timely and mentally prepared to wait for a confirmed appointment.
- Make a proper introduction that includes the organizational affiliation and its location.
- Foster a dialogue with administrative assistants, legislative aides, and other staffers. These connections can be helpful for dealing with the current issue and any future ones.
- Stay on script. Try not to ramble or get off track.
- Admit not knowing the answer to a given question, but promise to get the answer if possible.
- Complete the homework. Be prepared to speak intelligently about the issue and know something about the elected official—committee appointments, stances on issues etc.
- Know the number, name, sponsor, and cosponsor of the related bill(s) and something about the bill(s).
- Ask direct questions, such as whether the representative will support a given position. The goal is to get a commitment.
- Express appreciation for meeting the elected official.
- Take notes and refer to the notes later.

Don't:

- Express uncontrolled anger or speak in an offensive tone.
- Make statements that can be interpreted as aggressive.
- Make threats, such as, "I will remember this when you are up for reelection."
- Be fearful. Instead, speak with authority and confidence.
- Attempt to pass on loads of paperwork. Leave behind a one-page summary.

Things to Keep in Mind

- Elected officials enjoy having constituents visit their offices and take part in the democratic process.
- Elected officials like to be liked.
- In this relationship, the constituent is the employer and the elected official is the employee. Tax dollars pay the official's salary.

Effective Models for Justice Ministries

Minister Ayers, with the help of countless volunteers and under the leadership of Dr. Haynes, currently administers three models of engaging in social justice work at Friendship-West Baptist Church. Each model demonstrates how the three steps—community asset mapping, organizing, and mobilizing—are followed. The initiatives below are paradigms that demonstrate the use of social, intellectual, physical, financial, and political capital to achieve the ends of organizing and mobilizing for change.

Case Study: Wrongfully Convicted

The state of Texas leads the nation in the number of wrongful convictions. The Innocence Project, Dr. Jamie Page, Sociology professor at Texas A&M University Commerce, wrongfully convicted men, and communities of faith, along with other concerned community actors, have invested their time and energy in taking up the issue of wrongful convictions. Friendship-West, moreover, has actively advocated for change. Since 2001 twenty four men have been exonerated through DNA evidence.[2] Sadly, many other innocent men remain behind bars. Several laws are antiquated, and social structures have not been put in place to ensure a smooth transition back into the communities. In 2008 Friendship-West collaborated with other concerned groups in an attempt to change a broken system.

The following are highlights of their collaborative work:

HIGHLIGHTS

- Held educational/training sessions for staff pastors.

- Organized a legislative day for the Pastoral Affairs Team to advocate alongside the Innocence Project of Texas and the University of Texas at Arlington School of Social Work at the state capitol in Austin.

- Developed and implemented educational and inspirational public service announcements for FWBC News (internal news aired during worship service).

- Provided spiritual guidance to exonerees through staff pastors.

- Initiated an advocacy day for the congregation. Over 3,000 letters were signed and mailed to the Senate Committee on Criminal Justice in Austin.

- Collected a special offering and gave a monetary gift to exonerees. Consequently, an exoneree later donated $3,000 to FWBC.

Outcomes: Both the Timothy Cole Act of 2009 (increased compensation to exonerees upon exoneration) and Senate Bill 1681 (jailhouse testimony must have sound evidence to back up claims) were passed.

Case Study: Rescuing a Food Supply and Creating Opportunities

In the winter of 2008, Dr. Haynes challenged the staff and leadership of Friendship-West to envision how they would transform the community if the availability of resources was not an issue. Sensitive to the social, economic, and political situation of community residents, Min. Danielle Ayers believed a comprehensive movement rooted in social justice was necessary to recapture a communal mind-set and gain control of the local food supply. The Village Co-op was created to provide access to fresh fruit and vegetables, maintain environmental justice, stimulate the local economy, encourage social responsibility, and promote community sustainability. This was to be implemented though a farmers' market, community garden, and commercial-grade greenhouse.

The city of Dallas is divided into north and south by the Trinity River. South of the Trinity the quality of living is less than desirable. According to the Williams Research Institute's 2007 Wholeness Index, the southern sector leads the city in premature deaths. The rate of premature deaths is nearly twice (9,000) that of the city (4,900). Leading causes of death are chronic illnesses that can be prevented by a balanced food environment. Residents face nutritional challenges with no or distant grocery stores and fast food as an alternative. On average, neighborhoods with three or more grocery stores within a one-mile radius consist of 57 percent white residents compared to 12 percent African American residents. The report goes on to state, "Neighborhoods without grocery stores are predominantly low income and African American, with a concentration of no-grocery-store neighborhoods in southern Dallas, which has approximately 400,000 residents."[3]

With little or no economic development in the southern sector of Dallas, the Village Co-op seeks to stimulate economic activity that empowers and promotes cooperative economics. It is also concerned with a segment of the agricultural population that has been systematically locked out and/or has forgone developing the land due to lack of opportunity. With this in mind, a social justice approach was chosen to deal with the inequalities produced from past and present degenerative public policies, spoken and unspoken. The Village Co-op was designed to embrace challenges in the community and create opportunities. The foundation has rested on four pillars:

1. Public Health and Wellness

Food is essential to life. The promotion of health and wellness are essential. People who have access to fresh fruits and vegetables tend to have better eating habits and healthier lifestyles. Many chronic illnesses can be prevented through a balanced diet. Consumption of fruits and vegetables improves nutrition. With children having a part in caring for and harvesting the garden, many will have a greater knowledge of how fruits and vegetables are grown, of nutrition, and of how to develop healthier eating habits at a younger age.

2. Social Responsibility

The co-op creates teaching and entrepreneurial opportunities as well as space for global connections. A community garden offers an opportunity for children, youth, and adults to become educated in the areas of agricultural, biological, commercial, environmental, ecological, and natural science. Some will discover an entrepreneurial spirit. Others will develop leadership skills and gain a passion for teaching. Some will even become the next generations of farmers.

In addition, the Village Co-op promotes and nurtures human relationships and fosters dignity. The space in which the Village Co-op sits extends an open invitation for all to come. The grounds are a gathering place for individuals from various cultures and backgrounds to connect around common goals and interact. The Village Co-op includes a community garden and commercial-grade greenhouse. Both structures beautify the Oak Cliff neighborhood. The organizers hope that the dedicated space will provide therapy, healing, and self-sufficiency as well as foster a sense of ownership and pride by supplying families and communities with fresh fruits and vegetables while boosting a local economy and supporting small to medium farms. Individuals will have an opportunity to engage in fair trade.

3. Community Sustainability

Another outcome of the co-op is community sustainability through collaboration with designated community actors. Through the facilitation of the community garden and local farmers' market, organizers hope to grow a local economy; utilize social, human, intellectual, financial, and political capital; and obtain necessary resources. Gaining ownership of land, buildings, labor, and other resources to produce goods and services provides a solid foundation for the work to continue.

4. *Environmental Justice*

Working in conjunction with academia and government agencies, the project will employ the latest agricultural practices and energy-efficient technology based on sound academic research and experienced practitioners. With these goals in mind, the project organizers did the following:

HIGHLIGHTS

- Established partnerships with two land grant universities— Texas A&M University (A&M) and Prairie View A&M University (PV) extension programs.

- Connected with PV senior design studio in the School of Architecture. The following outcomes were produced: (1) A commercial-grade greenhouse was professionally designed under the leadership of Professor Curtis Davis. Friendship-West hosted a special design gallery and selected the top three greenhouse designs. A total of twenty students participated, and a financial reward was given to the top three winners. (2) Organizers connected with farmers in Oklahoma and Texas through PV and A&M.

- Partnered with the United States Department of Agriculture to develop the proper infrastructure for a regional food supply chain.

- Created and distributed community garden and farmers' market surveys to the congregation. They received approximately 2,500 responses.

- Held a co-op membership drive (150 families total).

- Held six-week community gardening classes facilitated by Dotty Woodson of Texas A&M University Extension Program. Ten members completed the course.

- Recruited ten consistent volunteers to work (plant, pull weeds, water, etc.) in the garden. The first planting included the following: turnips, onions, cabbage, broccoli, strawberries, blueberries, thyme, rosemary, oregano, carrots, cilantro, and more.

- Developed marketing material for co-op members, community, and church, including brochures, membership cards, T-shirts, banners, farmer-vendor packets, recyclable bags, and membership certificates.

- Held "What's Cooking at the Co-op?" where members sampled dishes made with produce and herbs grown in the garden.

- Worked with city council members to obtain necessary resources to expand the community garden.

Over the course of writing this book, the project has been preparing to continue one phase and enter another. We began offering a series of classes that focuses on health and nutrition accompanied by cooking demonstrations. We introduced a fair trade initiative. We now offer tea, coffee, and olive oil purchased from democratically run co-ops in Ethiopia, Uganda, El Salvador, Sri Lanka, the Darjeeling region of India, and Palestine.

Case Study: A Break in the Economy

In the southern sector of Dallas, there is a proliferation of payday and auto title loan businesses. On one street alone, there are seventeen locations. In the summer of 2010, an auto title loan business opened up just down the street from Friendship-West. Alarmed at the proliferation of predatory lenders in the community, Dr. Haynes brought the community together to deal with the harmful economic and social effects of these lending institutions. A statewide effort is now underway. Voices are being heard from the faith community, AARP, policy institutes, some elected officials, the United Way, and other community organizations. Under the leadership of Dr. Haynes and Minister Ayers, as of the writing of this book, the movement has accomplished the following:

HIGHLIGHTS

- Developed and distributed fact sheets to parishioners and to the community about how payday loans work. The fact sheets also listed alternatives to fill short-term cash needs.

- Collaborated with three other area churches to work collectively on the issues.

- Joined a citywide multidenominational and cultural coalition (Anti-Poverty Coalition) as well as a statewide 500 percent Interest Is Wrong campaign.

- Worked with state-wide organizations to further expand advocacy efforts.

- Researched how to adapt a best practices model for micro-financing.

- Met with local and state elected officials to stay abreast of proposed policy changes.

- Provided testimony before a Texas State House committee hearing as well as a local city council committee hearing.

- Held community meetings and press conferences to bring attention to such efforts and to educate citizens.

- Led a community march and rally.

- Circulated postcards to give individuals an opportunity to take a stand against lenders who operate through the Credit Service Organization loophole. The project received approximately three thousand postcards, which served as the voters' voice in Austin.

The collaborative efforts of the Anti Poverty Coalition, Texas Appleseed, Texas Life Commission, community organizers, countless concerned citizens and many others resulted in new policies at the municipal and state level. The City of Dallas passed two new ordinances (regulatory and zoning.) Loan terms and agreements are more just and businesses are precluded from clustering in economically disadvantaged communities. The state law now requires the payday/auto title industry be accountable to the Office of the Consumer Credit Commissioner.

The movement continues. As this chapter is being written, the aforementioned groups are preparing to advocate for more substantive legislation in the 83rd Texas Legislature in 2013. Several members of each organization have made visits to legislators and put in countless hours researching and preparing proposed legislation. In addition, FWBC is in the process of establishing a micro finance program, wherein small loans will be afforded to those who are susceptible to payday/auto title loans.

The examples and models presented in this chapter must be viewed in the social, economic, political, and historical context of Dallas. The resource section at the end of the book contains some examples of letters, press releases, and other documents the authors have used to organize and mobilize for justice.

Things to Keep In Mind

The Enemy in the Camp. Not everyone involved in any given movement is in it for the right reasons. Some are present to take back information to opposing forces, and others are present for personal gain. This is not good or bad; it is neutral. However, it is important to discern who is for social justice and who is against it. As Jesus found with Judas, his betrayer, the enemy in the camp can be used for the designed purpose. In fact, once the enemy has been identified, information can be disseminated accordingly.

Sprinter vs. Marathon Runner. Fighting for justice does not produce overnight sensations. Nor does it produce immediate outcomes or fruits of labor such as social service work may deliver. Hebrews 11 mentions that some biblical heroes of faith died without receiving the fulfillment of God's promise to them. In many instances, workers lay a solid foundation for others to build upon as we transition to different tasks or labors. Nevertheless, these workers will experience some victories along the way. Dr. King broke the economic backbone of Montgomery, Alabama, with the bus boycott. As a consequence, a change in public policy took place and segregation on buses became illegal. He did not, however, make it to the Promised Land. Regardless, the church must be committed to go the distance.

Opposition. Nehemiah certainly had his share of opposition. The initial waves of opposition included mockery and lies. Subsequent opposition was more intense and public. Opposition is good for the movement because it keeps the workers from becoming comfortable. It can also be the catalyst for change. In the case of the Triangle Shirtwaist Factory in the early twentieth century, primarily immigrant women laid down their lives in an effort to form a union in order to receive better working conditions and pay. The factory owners took extreme measures to crush their protest efforts, and no substantial changes were made. Unfortunately, 146 workers died when the factory burned down. The death toll was attributed to the poor conditions of the building and a possible locked exit door that prevented the women from escaping. This incident shook New York City. As a consequence, the New York legislature took action. Set working hours, standards for minimum wages, requirements for workplace conditions, and stronger child labor laws were some of the many changes.

Collaboration and/or Confrontation. When Jesus entered the temple and turned the tables over, the money changers were performing a legitimate and necessary function, but biblical scholars believe they were charging inflated rates. When engaging in community development/ organizing there are times when people likewise will be in positions to perform legitimate functions, but at some point the functions will turn against those on the margins or in the community.

This is when collaboration and confrontation can become tools used to maximize efforts to achieve desired outcome. Social justice ministries must make the decision to collaborate or confront based on wisdom and careful assessment of the situation and the political atmosphere surrounding it. Some issues by nature will call for confrontation and others for collaboration. In some cases, it may be necessary to begin with confrontation and end with collaboration. At other times collaboration will be the best option.

This chapter has presented practical guidelines for moving from inside the local church into the community and for organizing the community for social justice work. It has focused on assessment, taking the results of the assessment to the people (inside and outside the church), and garnering people power for change. A number of case studies have been presented along with checklists, questionnaires, and "things to keep in mind." The social justice ministry can now begin planning how to maintain the foundation that has been laid and the walls that have been repaired. This is the topic of the next chapter.

///////////

NOTES

1. Frederick D. Haynes III, "From Vision to Action: Principles of Organizing a Theologically Grounded and Vision-Driven Church to Effectively Implement Ministries at the Local, National and Global Levels," in *Blow the Trumpet in Zion! Global Vision and Action for the 21st Century Black Church*, ed. Iva E. Carruthers, Frederick D. Haynes III, and Jeremiah A. Wright Jr. (Minneapolis: Augsburg Fortress, 2005), 24.

2. See http://www.innocenceproject.org/Content/Dallas_County_Cases_Where_DNA_Has_Proven_Innocence.php.

3. Nathan Berg and James Murdoch (2007). *Access to Grocery Stores and Food Security in Dallas*. Center for Urban Economics at the University of Texas at Dallas, 2, 5.

CHAPTER 5
Sustaining the Work

//

A familiar statement in the community of faith is that salvation is free but ministry costs. The reality is that engaging in social justice work requires funding. This chapter explores options for funding and reemphasizes the importance of sound financial infrastructures. However, some economists have said that the economy today is in worse condition than it was during the Great Depression of the 1930s. This dismal economy is having an impact on contributions to churches, and it is also having an impact on other charitable organizations that perform essential community services and that stand for justice. Thus any advice concerning creative strategies for fund development is most welcome to social justice ministries in local churches.

With that in mind, Min. Ayers interviewed Rev. Dameon Madison, pastor of stewardship and development at Friendship-West Baptist Church, to get ideas based on his experiences with laying financial infrastructures. Previously Madison worked as a project coordinator for the Nashville Minority Business Agency, raising funds for its annual gala with a budget of $110k. The sponsorship was comprised of both individual and corporate donors. Madison later served as youngest vice president of advancement at Talladega College in Talladega, Alabama. There he was responsible for managing the director of development, the grants director, corporate relations, and Title III funding.

In the following interview, Madison discusses his current responsibilities at Friendship-West and provides ideas for sustaining justice work.

Ayers: What are your primary duties as the pastor of stewardship and development?

Madison: Internally, I am responsible for maintaining and growing the giving base of church members. Externally, I am responsible for establishing and maintaining relationships with philanthropists, foundations, corporations, and nonprofit organizations. All of this is for the purpose of securing funding to support the ministry.

Ayers: In the megachurch context, how do you create an environment of giving and connect the people to the ministry and vision of Friendship-West?

Madison: The Sunday morning worship service is the place where we maximize our opportunity to connect with the people. Throughout the week, the task is a bit more challenging. Some people are not necessarily connected to the church as much as they are connected to a personality.

Then some people are casual givers. Others are more mature and understand the biblical principle of giving their tithes and offerings. To inspire giving, it is important to share information. Therefore we often tell the story of Friendship-West. We tell the story of ministry successes and inform people of ministry initiatives. This enables potential donors (internal and external) to see the work we do and how it has impacted and transformed lives in the community. I would also add that this should be done in higher education and in other nonprofits that depend on funding.

Ayers: How does one determine who is likely to allocate funding to justice work?

Madison: Pastoral priority is critical. The senior pastor must lead the way. Not all pastors are socially driven. So it is important to have a detailed and itemized budget. Planning should be based on financial resources balanced against operational cost.

Ayers: Matthew 6:21 says, "Where your treasure is, there will your heart be also" [KJV]. So is it safe to say a church's budget tells what ministry is important to it?

Madison: Yes!

Ayers: How are donations received, and are donors able to select specific areas where they would like for contributions to go?

Madison: Contributions are primarily received through offering envelopes. We do have the option of online giving as well. In terms of
options to designate where contributions may go, we simply make
the following options available both online and with envelopes:
Tithes and Offering, Haiti, and a fill-in-the-blank. It is best to limit the
number of options to keep it basic and simple.

Ayers: What is the importance of having a fill-in-the-blank option?

Madison: This gives people the opportunity to connect with what they
are passionate about.

Ayers: Outside of Tithes and Offering, what are some other options?

Madison: Federal grants, foundation awards, and major gifts (philanthropists) are additional funding sources. I would also add that a
church/organization must have the proper infrastructure [refer back
to chapter 3]. This includes creating sub-nonprofits so funds are not
comingled with the church. High-profile givers will give to the work
they are passionate about and if they like the work you are doing.

Ayers: What initial steps should a church/organization take to secure
grants?

Madison: I would recommend three things. Number one, a church
should hire a grant specialist if the budget allows for it. A church can
also hire a consultant to identify funds. It is important to make sure
the individual has a proven track record in grant writing. This person
must be able to convey your organization's mission and information
about your project in a clear and concise manner. In addition, the
grant proposal must have correct grammar and punctuation. Grants
submitted with errors and not of a professional caliber will not be
considered.

Number two, churches should seek out resources from the Center for Nonprofit Management (management training and grants/
foundation resources), Grants.gov (federal grants), the Christian
Funding Directory, and BIG Online are some starter resources. And
lastly, I would recommend that churches become part of the Foundation Center by logging onto http://foundationcenter.org/.

Ayers: Talk a little bit about the importance of external partnerships.

Madison: External partnerships link you to a network that can open
doors you may not otherwise be able to access. You either have to

know people who have assets and are affluent, or you have to know people who are influential who can gain access to individuals with assets and who are affluent.

Ayers: Building and sustaining a solid fund development program, creating a stream of funding, and building relationships takes time. Would you agree?

Madison: Yes! It is a slow process. If one takes the time to lay a solid foundation, it will pay off and be sustainable. For example, the $1 million donation I received for Talladega College was a four-year process. Relationship building is always the cornerstone.

Ayers: What is another benefit of external partnerships as it relates to grant funding?

Madison: Having partnerships with organizations that are doing the same work or who may fill in parts of the work are looked upon very favorably.

Ayers: Would you like to share any last thoughts?

Madison: Yes. I would suggest the following: Number one: do your research. Dedicate at least one day of the week to research grants. Keep in mind that every grant will not match your organization. Number two: do not match funds to the work. Match the work to the funds. Number three: rely on your creativity. Create opportunities for people to give toward the work. Use technology to your advantage. Lastly, make sure the senior pastor, executive director, or board president has a buy-in on the work/program/initiative.

Ayers: You have shared a wealth of information and provided some suggestions about infrastructure as it relates to sustaining the work. Would you recommend this same framework for a church of any size?

Madison: Yes. The same framework can be implemented based on the scale and scope the church is able to accommodate.

Ayers: Can you recommend a book on the subject of sustaining the work through giving?

Madison: Yes. *Stewardship in African-American Churches: A New Paradigm* by Melvin Amerson.

Rev. Dameon Madison has underscored the idea that receiving contributions and outside funding are parts of sustaining the work of social justice. The proper placement of personnel and the establishment of processes and procedures are critical as well. Managing church financials, staff, and external relationships must be approached in a manner that upholds integrity and promotes transparency. The remainder of this chapter presents some best practices for implementing and conducting a smooth operation.

Important Issues

The church is at its best when it is engaged in the work of transformation. Social justice ministry speaks on behalf of those who live on the margins, giving a voice to those whose cries are not heard and bringing permanent relief to those who are suffering. The church is obligated to take seriously the church's walk with Jesus as it seeks to model his ministry by living out the biblical mandate to do justice based on Luke 4:18.

In sustaining the work, it is important to keep in mind the quote by Nelson Mandela offered in chapter 3 of this book: "The freedom struggle is not merely a question of making speeches, holding meetings, passing resolutions, and sending deputations, but of meticulous organization, militant mass action, and above all the willingness to suffer and sacrifice."[1]

To extend this thought, when the church not only gets involved in justice work but allocates resources to staff and individuals in the role of social justice advocates, it sends a message that it is committed to being a prophetic witness even if that means "swimming against the tide." A wide range of benefits is involved in having a staff person to head a specific social justice ministry area in the local church. Such a position can serve as a clearing-house for disseminating information, gathering the community, and mobilizing for action. In other words, this local church social justice ministry office can serve as the conscience of the state.

Now a few more thoughts are worth mentioning.

- Accountability and Integrity (Leadership Structure): The integrity of a movement, ministry, or organization is key. People need to be able to depend on and trust in those who declare that they are fighting for the people. A lack of integrity can cause people to feel that they have no recourse and no outlet, even from the ones who claim to help them.

- Communication: Communication is the sending and receiving of messages. Any relationship and any ministry or movement will be compromised by unhealthy communication. Healthy communication requires open, honest dialogue, and not dictation. Communication requires also that each side be willing to actively listen to the other in order to be fully aware of what is at stake and what has to be done.

- Research: The importance of in-depth research cannot be stressed enough. Without research, any movement will be stagnant and stifled. Without research, one cannot be fully apprised of what is at stake. Research gives the ammunition with which to fight for fairness and justice.

This chapter has focused on the critical need for financial infrastructures to support social justice ministry. It has outlined creative strategies for seeking funding from outside the church and from within the church. Central to the chapter is an interview with Rev. Dameon Madison, pastor of stewardship and development at Friendship-West Baptist Church. This chapter has highlighted the importance of accountability, integrity, communication, and research. Next we will explore resources for social justice issues that churches across the country are currently facing.

//////
NOTE

1. Nelson Mandela, as quoted in Dennis A. Jacobsen, *Doing Justice: Congregations and Community Organizing* (Minneapolis: Fortress, 2001), 79.

CHAPTER 6

Considering Common Justice Issues and Strategies

In communities across the country, there are some common issues that burden social justice ministries and those they serve. In this chapter we will explore three of those issues: mass incarceration, food deserts in communities of the poor, and predatory lending. We will offer direction and resources for educating about these issues and addressing them as they exist within a variety of community contexts simultaneously.

Mass Incarceration

In May 2008, Bruce Western of Harvard University said, "We are living in an era of mass imprisonment that has transformed a generation of young black men who form the core of a permanently disadvantaged population. The prison is now important, not chiefly for its effects on crime, but for its effects on social and economic inequality."[1] David Garland, editor of *Mass Imprisonment: Social Causes and Consequences,* defines mass imprisonment as "a rate of imprisonment . . . that is markedly above the historical and comparative norm for societies of this type. . . . Imprisonment ceases to be the incarceration of individual offenders and becomes the systematic imprisonment of whole groups of the population."[2]

In no uncertain terms, the use of the criminal justice system as a means of social control is killing communities. Consider the following facts:

- America has more than two million citizens behind bars, which is the highest amount per capita in the world.[3]

- "One in three young African American men will serve time in prison if current trends continue, and in some cities, more than half of all young adult black men are currently under correctional control—in prison or jail, on probation or parole."[4]

- "More African Americans adults are under correctional control today—in prison or jail, on probation or parole—than were enslaved in 1850, a decade before the civil war began."[5]

These statistics and many more that support them are indicative of what attorney Michelle Alexander has termed "The New Jim Crow." According to Alexander, just as the Jim Crow of the South relegated African Americans to an underclass and undercaste system that denied certain basic rights because of who they were, the New Jim Crow denies the formerly incarcerated the right to vote and the right to jury service, exposes them to housing discrimination, and denies them food stamps. In essence, it denies them basic citizenship rights. It is a systematic way to keep a certain class of people and a certain race of people locked within an undercaste system.[6] This is especially so when legislation has criminalized nonviolent drug offenses. Many of the inmates are nonviolent offenders who need help and not prison time. Nevertheless, people of color tend to get jail time, while those of European descent get therapy. Therein lies the breakdown and disparity in the numbers game that just doesn't add up.[7]

The privatization of prisons by companies such as Corrections Corporation of America and the GEO group, whose stocks are traded on Wall Street, literally has turned prisons not into a place of rehabilitation but mass incarceration for the purpose of profit. And so once again, just as in chattel slavery, there is free labor to build an economy.

Even deeper is the discussion about the prison industrial complex, which is also fed by the failure of the educational system, especially the public schools around the country. A number of organizations are tackling this issue. For assistance in fighting mass incarceration, social justice ministries can contact the following organizations and secure the related resources:

- Samuel DeWitt Proctor Conference[8]
- Children's Defense Fund, *Cradle to Prison Pipeline Project*[9]
- The Black Community Crusade for Children[10]
- *The New Jim Crow* by Michelle Alexander[11]
- *Ministry with Prisoners & Families* by W. Wilson Goode Sr., Charles E. Lewis Jr., and Harold Dean Trulear[12]

Food Deserts in Communities of the Poor

In the autumn of 2008, Harry Ellerson of University Park, Illinois, was diagnosed with multiple myeloma, a cancer of the plasma cells in the bone marrow. In addition to the other forms of treatment ascribed to Mr. Ellerson, he was instructed by his physicians to eat only fresh fruits and vegetables. However, in University Park, there were no grocery stores, nor was there an opportunity to get fresh fruits and vegetables. University Park sits in what the USDA has termed a "food desert." Harry Ellerson passed away in early 2009. Multiple myeloma was a major contributor. However, another factor in Mr. Ellerson's demise was the fact that he lived in a food desert.

In the 2008 Farm Bill, the term *food desert* is defined as an "area in the United States with limited access to affordable and nutritious food, particularly such an area composed of predominantly lower income neighborhoods and communities."[13] In food deserts, the lack of access to fresh fruits and vegetables and other healthy foods coupled with the high prices of basic staples at convenience stores has an adverse effect on the health of people with low incomes in low-income neighborhoods. It is easy to suggest that someone get into their car and drive to the nearest grocery store. It is even easier to suggest that someone get on public transportation to go to a grocery store, farmers' market, or similar establishment. However, what if one can't afford a car? What if an area has limited access to public transportation? Both of these factors make the reality of living in a food desert a challenging reality of existence.

While it is important to choose to eat healthy foods in order to support healthy living, too often, particularly for people who live in rural and low-income areas, foods are chosen for them. By this, I mean that the foods which are sent to grocery stores, corner stores, and the like are not as healthy and filled with nutritional value as the foods made available in communities of wealth and privilege. Therefore, the choice of foods that are made available is relegated to primarily fast food and snacks from corner stores and gas stations.

In addition to food accessibility, we must also examine food affordability. The definition of food desert itself speaks not only of a dearth of accessibility but also of affordability. Too often healthy foods are reserved for those who have the means to pay for them, which tends to make access to affordable foods a privilege and not a right. This lack of choice and lack of access to healthy foods leads to health concerns for a population already suffering from poverty. Increased rates of obesity, coupled with chronic health concerns such as diabetes, heart disease, hypertension, and the like, can be linked to the profusion of food deserts. Food accessibility is thus a social justice issue.

Predatory Lending

Payday and auto title loan businesses exist primarily in disadvantaged communities—and in large numbers there. They add no economic value to the community and do not contribute to the tax base. The state of Texas is in the midst of a movement to close the Credit Service Organization loophole (CSO), by which some companies register as CSOs when in fact they are storefront lending institutions. Through this loophole, the businesses do not operate under set rules and regulations as do other lenders. They can therefore charge excessive fees and interest rates as high as 700 percent on a $500 loan. Selena Xie of Texas Impact states, "The result is that Texans that have borrowed money in a crisis end up trapped in a loan, regularly making payments, but never reducing the amount owed. A $300 loan taken out in a financial emergency often costs $850 to pay back. Faith compels social justice ministries to speak out against this type of practice."[14]

When a community is saturated with payday and auto title loan stores, other forms of viable and sustainable economic development projects will not locate in these areas. This process can be convoluted and confusing to many people who enter into loan agreements. Often people seek payday and/or auto title loans when they find themselves in a desperate situation with no other alternatives for small short-term loans.

The unjust business practices of the industry in Texas compelled various community advocates to take action. A collaborative effort among faith communities, service organizations, community organizers, and public policy institutes yielded modest changes in public policy. These changes resulted in zoning and regulatory ordinances in the City of Dallas and accountability at the state level. The Texas payday and auto title loan industry is extremely powerful and equipped with lobbyists to represent their interest at the state capital in Austin.

Powerful industries and lobbyists exist in most communities. Some of the tactics used in Texas can be utilized to address other types of industries. The first step is to build a coalition to support a common agenda and messaging. The second step is to create and communicate a compelling narrative of individuals negatively impacted by industry practices. Their stories must be told to decision makers and the community at large. For example, we collected stories of Texans who found themselves trapped in a cycle of debt. The stories were shared during senate committee hearings. The stories were also shared with congregations and media. Sharing personal stories humanizes the issue.

The third step is to identify elected officials who may support your efforts. Once potential supporters are identified, a coordinated effort to make office visits must take place among the coalition. In our statewide efforts, coalition members committed to visiting targeted elected officials in their respective districts. It will be important and beneficial to present your case based on facts and well-thought-out proposed changes. The fourth step is to develop a social media strategy. And lastly, prepare for setbacks and be flexible to make necessary adjustments.

Tactics and Tools

Here we will explore a few tactics and tools that can be used to pursue various social justice issues.

Talking Points

A key component of the ministry of social justice is research. Data must be investigated and shared in a clear and concise manner. From your research, create a set of talking points that highlight the key components of the issue at hand. This will keep your allies on point and on the same page so that all involved are speaking from one set of standards. A good set of talking points will do the following:

- Define the issue.
- Dictate how the issue affects those concerned.
- Devise how the responsible parties and powers that be can bring the issue to an equitable end.
- Direct those concerned about how to proceed in light of the defined issues.

Letter Campaigns

Letters are always an excellent mode of action. As a rule of thumb, when addressed to elected officials, those officials associate one letter with ten voters. To get the maximum number of letters signed and sent to the appropriate parties, a good idea is to have the letters signed during a worship service as an act of worship. (For nonreligious organizations, a letter may be signed during any meeting where a mass of the membership is in attendance.)

Letters can be distributed by ushers either as worshippers enter the sanctuary or as the pastor calls for the letters during a set time in the service. Doing this accomplishes at least two things. First, it shows parishioners that taking action for justice in the form of letters is a way to worship God. Second, it allows a good number of people to participate in an action that also yields a good number of signatures.

Below are some components of a good letter-writing campaign. These components can be used when writing individually or when writing to be distributed for signatures by organizations or congregations.

- No more than one page
- Proper address
- Paragraph one
  —Why I write
  —Issue definition
- Middle paragraph(s)
  —Facts supporting the case and the author's side of the argument
- Final paragraph
  —The author's request or demand for the actions of the addressed parties
  – What is requested
  – By when a response is expected
  – Contact information
- Closing

A strong complement to a letter-writing campaign may include phone calls, emails, faxes, and a social networking campaign using tools such as Facebook and Twitter.

People Power

There is strength in numbers and in meeting people face-to-face. Therefore do the following:

- Meet with elected officials.
- Attend meetings of importance.
- Conduct demonstrations.

Mass Meetings and Rallies

There is no substitute for people power preventing business as usual from proceeding. Strategic action with a specified goal toward a desired outcome must be planned prior to proceeding.

Mass meetings and rallies serve two very distinct yet related purposes—education and inspiration.

- *Education.* Mass meetings and rallies, first of all, serve as a form of education. During mass meetings, leaders can educate the masses about the issues. Information can be disseminated, instructions can be given, and directions can be delivered.

- *Inspiration.* During mass meetings, people can also be inspired to continue in the face of opposition. When people see that they are not walking the road alone, they are inspired to continue the fight.

Spread the Word

In this chapter, we have highlighted some social justice issues that are plaguing communities throughout the country—mass incarceration, food deserts, and predatory lending. We have also suggested strategies that communities can use to address these issues and have provided guidelines for how social justice ministries can lead these community efforts.

NOTES

1. Bruce Western, *Punishment and Inequality in America*, African American Labor Leaders Economic Summit on Labor & Religion. Lecture conducted from Harvard University, Cambridge, MA, May 8, 2008.

2. David Garland, *Mass Imprisonment: Social Causes & Consequences*. Thousand Oak, CA: SAGE Publications, 2001.

3. PEW Center on the States, *One in 100: Behind Bars in America 2008* (Washington, DC: PEW Charitable Trusts, 2008), 5.

4. Michelle Alexander, *The New Jim Crow: Mass Incarceration in the Age of Colorblindness* (New York: New Press, 2010), 9.

5. Ibid., 179.

6. Ibid., 178.

7. Ibid., 97.

8. Samuel DeWitt Proctor Conference website: http://www.sdpconference.info/.

9. Children's Defense Fund website: http://www.childrensdefense.org/.

10. Black Community Crusade for Children website: http://www.childrensdefense.org/programs-campaigns/black-community-crusade-for-children-II/.

11. See note 4 above and the New Press website: http://thenewpress.com/. A study guide to the book *The New Jim Crow*, for use in church-based educational settings, can be purchased from the Samuel DeWitt Proctor Conference website, cited in note 8 above.

12. W. Wilson Goode Sr., Charles E. Lewis Jr., and Harold Dean Trulear, *Ministry with Prisoners & Families* (Valley Forge, PA: Judson Press, 2011).

13. Food, Conservation, and Energy Act of 2008, Title VI, sec. 7527, United States Department of Agriculture.

14. Selena Xie, "Texas Faith for Fair Lending: Religious Leaders Call for Reform in Payday Lending Regulation," Texas Impact, texasimpact.org, March 21, 2011.

CONCLUSION
Staying on the Wall

///

Every step toward the goal of justice requires sacrifice, struggling, and suffering; the tireless exertions and passionate concern of dedicated individuals.

—Martin Luther King Jr.

In the context of social justice, it is important to uphold three guiding principles. First, actions should be public and collective. It is important to keep in mind that activities are political, economic, and group-related. Second, actions are geared toward permanent changes. Social justice ministry engages in policy-driven direct actions and engages with elected officials and in community partnerships. Lastly, such actions are aimed at resolving structural injustices—that is, they seek to be transformational in nature.

The church has a unique opportunity to partner with various community actors and organizations to address issues with which people live between Sundays. The church can also offer an irreplaceable voice in the world when it confronts injustice. It is not an easy task, and it does not come without long days, lonely nights, and even confrontation with great opposition—inside and outside the church. The good news is that the church is never without witness. Hebrews 12:1 says Christians are surrounded by a cloud of saints who have sojourned this way before us. It only requires taking a roll call of the storied past of the black church in this country to discover those who stood courageously and spoke truth to power against great odds.

In Matthew 10:16, Jesus gives a formula for engaging in justice work. There he says, "Behold I send you forth as sheep in the midst of wolves: be . . . wise as serpents, and harmless as doves" (KJV). In Dr. Martin Luther King Jr.'s *Strength to Love*, we find a sermon he preached from this text entitled "A Tough Mind and a Tender Heart."[1] The formula calls for critical thinking, educating oneself and others about the issues, and making sound judgments about how to move forward strategically with intentionality and a heart of compassion. Social justice ministries are without a doubt sheep going up against a wolfish system, but we have the reassurance that we have a Good Shepherd whose rod and staff comfort us. Further, we are also reminded that though often we labor in the valley under formidable threats, goodness and mercy follow us (Psalm 23).

It is our hope that this book has provided a framework from which to construct and sustain justice ministry. We pray this brief volume sends forth social justice workers with words like those from the Charles Wesley hymn:

> A charge to keep I have, a God to glorify,
> A never dying soul to save, and fit it for the sky.
> To serve this present age, my calling to fulfill;
> O may it all my pow'rs engage, to do my Master's will."

Peace and justice!

///////

NOTE

1. Martin Luther King Jr., *Strength to Love* (Philadelphia: Fortress, 1981).

AFTERWORD

A Charge to Keep—
A Gift to Give

///

*Awake youth of the land and accept this noble challenge of sal-
vaging the strong ship of civilization by the anchors of right, justice, and love. . . . let us resolve that for the welfare of the whole,
for the good of all, for the uplift of the fallen humanity, for the
extension of Christ's kingdom on earth . . . there shall be no turn-
ing back . . . we will strike against evil, strife and war.*

—Ella Baker,
excerpt from valedictorian speech, 1927[1]

Upon graduating from Shaw University in 1927, Ella Baker led a
life of sacrificial leadership and became one of the most influential
and beloved human rights activists of the twentieth century. The
spirit of Ella Baker permeates the purpose, power, and promise of
*To Serve This Present Age: Social Justice Ministries in the Black
Church.* Danielle Ayers and Reginald Williams Jr. have creatively
woven and penned their personal convictions, theological reflections, and ministry experiences into an educational and practical
resource for clergy and lay leaders.

By their work, the anchors of right, justice, and love are placed
in context of today's social, political, and spiritual realities, so

inimical to the well-being of African-descended people and other oppressed persons the world over.

By their creativity, we are challenged to effect new models of shared and sacrificial leadership to be nonconformist agitators, thinking globally and acting locally.

By their exhortation, we are reminded that God's way calls upon us to seek the common good, to live in the spirit of Ubuntu, and to treat the people's needs as a sacred trust.

In these times, their call to the black church, clergy and laity, and all people of goodwill is indeed a call "to strike against evil, strife and war." If not us, then whom?

Scripture says to "keep the charge of the LORD, so that you may not die" (Leviticus 8:35, NKJV). I am grateful for the living ministries of Minister Danielle Ayers and Rev. Reginald Williams. I am grateful that they have not squandered the opportunities they have been afforded to serve under and learn from two of the most prophetic preachers-pastors-activists of this century. *To Serve This Present Age* is a gift to give as the prophetic witness of the black church seeks to proclaim and reclaim its footing in this present age.

Iva E. Carruthers, PhD
General Secretary
Samuel DeWitt Proctor Conference

//////

NOTE

1. Source: Ransby, Barbara. Ella Baker & The Black Freedom Movement.

EPILOGUE
A Charge to Keep in This Present Age

The Reverend Jesse Jackson has insightfully illustrated the need for attacking injustice by suggesting that if one has a size 10 foot, but they have been made to wear a size 8 shoe, eventually the wearer will develop a painful corn. It may be nice to give the person in pain medication for the corn, but it is necessary and prudent to change shoes because the issue is structural. It's one thing to soothe the symptom, but it's righteous to correct the cause.

Minister Danielle Ayers and Rev. Reginald Williams Jr. have charged people of faith in particular, and persons of goodwill in general, to not settle for dispensing the medication of charity to communities that have been victimized by structural injustice, but to engage in a prophetic ministry of social justice that fights to change the "shoe." When we feed the hungry during special holidays, it may comfort our conscience and temporarily alleviate the pain of poverty, but the structures that create poverty and hunger remain in place and suffering people have to be satisfied with "medication" until the next holiday. When we visit prisons and lead worship experiences, it may give the visiting prison ministries a good feeling, but the structural injustice that has escalated the prison population, especially with African American women and men, will remain in place and only give the prison ministry a larger "congregation" to preach to the next visit. Ayers and Williams show and tell us how to change the "shoe" of injustice.

Ayers and Williams are prophetic practitioners of the charge they have issued and this challenging charge reflects their brilliant and passionate commitment to "speaking truth to power" while empowering the powerless and addressing issues of injustice. This wake-up call to the church and all people of principle is practically helpful and insightfully inspirational. It comes from the well of wisdom borne out of their respective experiences on the front lines as they have taken the gospel from the sanctuary to the streets and to corporate suites, challenging institutional iniquity and structural sin.

I'm sure that Amos, the minor prophet from the eighth century BCE with a major message, would be excited reading how his poetic imagery of justice rolling "down as waters and righteousness as an ever flowing stream" is a practical possibility for ministries in the twenty-first century. Jesus, the Christ, may well say "well done" to Ayers and Williams for showing us how the Word may become flesh in ministries that serve as a voice for the voiceless and minister to the least of these.

If you refuse to hit the snooze button on this wake-up call, then the meaningful message, practical pointers, and convicting charge in *To Serve This Present Age* will prevent this book from gathering dust on some bookshelf. You will return again and again to this rich resource that will inform and inspire you and your ministry to make a difference in the lives of the disinherited and the systems that oppress by "changing the shoes" of injustice.

Frederick Douglass Haynes III
Pastor, Friendship–West Baptist Church
Dallas, Texas

Resource Guide

//

This appendix provides sample resources that can be adapted for use in various contexts. They show what social justice ministries can do. The following samples are included:

- Fact Sheet
- Press Release
- Letter to Committee Chair
- Invitation to Candidates to Participate in a Collaborative Political Forum
- Sample Letters Addressing a Variety of Topics
- Additional Resources

Sample Fact Sheet

Fact Sheet: Children's Health Insurance Program (CHIP)

Background

The Texas CHIP program provides insurance coverage for working families. CHIP is for families who earn too much money to qualify for Medicaid yet cannot afford to purchase private insurance for their children. CHIP provides eligible children with coverage for a full range of health services, including regular checkups, immunizations, prescription drugs, lab tests, X-rays, hospital visits, and more.

Facts

- Texas has the highest rate of uninsured children in the nation, with 20.2 percent lacking coverage, compared to 11.6 percent nationally. (Source: 2006 U.S. Census)

- More than 80 percent of uninsured children have at least one working parent.

- Of the 1.5 million uninsured Texas children, 850,000 are eligible for but not enrolled in CHIP or Children's Medicaid.

- More than one out of every five Texas children (21.8%) lives in poverty.

- President George Bush vetoed the first $35-billion Federal S-CHIP expansion when it crossed his desk, complaining that it covered middle-class children at the expense of the poor. On December 12, 2008, he vetoed the bill again, even though it would have provided coverage for over 10 million children.

The Goal

To advocate for, educate, and enroll every eligible Dallas child in Medicaid/CHIP.

Phase I Recommendations: "Start a Conversation"

In an effort to make an impact, the following actions need to be taken:

- Distribute flyers to youth and children and to their families.
- Identify a "Champion for Children."
- Continue to advocate on behalf of uninsured youth and children.
- Include CHIP outreach as part of a health fair or 2008 church event.
- Identify uninsured youth and children within the church/community.
- Include information in bulletins on the FWBC News, on the website, and on the radio.

Sample Press Release

For Immediate Release:

Contact: _____ Phone Number _____

Economic Impact of Housing, Journalism Advocacy, Criminal Justice/Societal Reentry, and Haynes' Bill of Rights for the Poor on Summit Platform

Media and Criminal Justice/Prison Experts Headline Second Faith Summit on Poverty

United States Congresswoman Maxine Waters (D-Ca.) and Dr. Frederick D. Haynes III, senior pastor of the Friendship-West Baptist Church in Dallas, Texas, have joined forces again to host the 2nd Annual Faith Summit on Poverty on March 30 and 31, 2007, at the Friendship-West Worship and Conference Center, 2020 W. Wheatland Road, Dallas. The central theme and goal is to *enlighten and equip* citizens to mobilize their state, local, and federal politicians toward a meaningful, updated, and earnest War on Poverty!

The Texas House of Representatives held a hearing on House Bill 947, the Bill of Rights for the Underprivileged, on March 15, 2007. Representative Yvonne Davis of Legislative District 111 sponsored the bill, which came out of the 2006 Faith Summit on Poverty, authored by Dr. Haynes. This legislation will institute a policy statement for the State of Texas that reinforces basic rights every Texan, including the underprivileged of our society, should enjoy.

Town Hall Meeting

Saturday March 31, 2007, 9 a.m.–12 p.m.

A panel discussion featuring nationally acclaimed speakers will be moderated by U.S. Representative Maxine Waters and Dr. Haynes. The panel will include:

- Dr. Michael Eric Dyson, author and professor
- Dick Gregory, comedian and activist
- Vaughn Irons, national director of expanding markets, Freddie Mac
- Brian Collier, director, Texas Board of Pardons
- Dr. Johnny Ray Youngblood, pastor, St. Paul Community Baptist Church, Brooklyn, New York
- Royce West, Texas state senator
- Craig Watkins, Dallas County district attorney
- Valencia Nash, justice of the peace, Precinct 1, Place 2

AT&T Community Job Expo

Saturday, 10 a.m.–2 p.m. (Running Currently with Town Hall Meeting)

AT&T will lead more than 60 employers and a consortium of Job Training, Trade School, and Institutions of Continuing Education to deliver onsite Job Fair and Career Training opportunities. A plus for job seekers is onsite/online application completion. Other sponsors include Comerica Bank, Citibank, and KKDA and KRNB Radio Stations.

Sample Letter to Committee Chair

Sunday, March 8, 2009

The Honorable John Whitmire
P.O. Box 12068
Capitol Station
Austin, TX 78711

Dear Criminal Justice Committee Chairperson Whitmire:

Friendship-West Baptist Church (FWBC) is located in Dallas, Texas, and is pastored by Dr. Frederick D. Haynes III. FWBC is dedicated to going beyond the walls of the church and being strong advocates for positive substantive policies. We also strongly believe in giving a voice to the voiceless and the most vulnerable in society. In the fall of 2008, we had the privilege of meeting with some Dallas County exonerees. After hearing their stories, we were moved with compassion. As a result, we held a meeting with Attorney Clay Graham and Dr. Jamie Page of the University of Texas at Arlington (UTA) School of Social Work. Out of that meeting we connected with the Innocence Project of Texas.

In February 2009 we traveled to the state capital to join forces with the Innocence Project of Texas, UTA School of Social Work, exonerees, and several concerned Texas citizens. We walked the corridors of the state capital knocking on Senate and House of Representatives doors to discuss the problems with and possible solutions to wrongful convictions. We were warmly received. Out of this experience, we returned to FWBC and began a Sunday morning series on wrongful convictions, highlighting the exonerees and possible policies geared toward eliminating wrongful convictions. After a month-long emphasis, we concluded with a "Call to Action" on Sunday, March 8, 2009. This "Call to Action" challenged all of us to sign a letter of support for Senate Bill (SB) 117, authored by Senator Rodney Ellis, and to challenge committee members to vote for SB117.

We are excited about the work of the Criminal Justice Committee and remain hopeful that SB 117 will make it out of the committee. Thank you for receiving over 2,700 letters enclosed in the box as a collective voice of those in attendance at the Sunday morning worship service on March 8, 2009.

Regards,
Danielle Ayers, Minister of Social Justice

Enclosures
cc: Senator Royce West

Invitation to Candidates to Participate in a Collaborative Political Forum

League of Women Voters
of Dallas Education Fund

August 5, 2010

Dear _____:

On behalf of the League of Women Voters of Dallas Education Fund and Friendship-West Baptist Church, it is my pleasure to invite you to participate in a Meet the Candidates Forum for _____ of Dallas County. We are excited to provide the place and opportunity for Dallas citizens to hear your vision for the county.

This forum will be held from ___ to ___ p.m. on Thursday, October 14, 2010, at Friendship-West Baptist Church, 2020 W. Wheatland Road, Dallas. Please be at the site 15 minutes prior to the start in order to adjust microphones and receive further instructions.

Attached you will find two documents:

- The first document is the **Candidate Reply Form,** indicating your participation in the forum. Please **return by September 1.**

- The second document is the League of Women Voters **Forum Policy and Format.** Please read and adhere to the participation criteria.

In an effort to maximize citizen participation, **trained volunteers will be monitoring a live chat forum onsite, screening questions, and providing feedback from viewers online.** Additionally, each candidate will have a designated space for literature distribution. Please make certain someone from your campaign is available to work your table.

If you have any questions, please call the League office at 214-688-4125 or Danielle Ayers at Friendship-West Baptist Church at 972-228-5226.

You make democracy work when you inform voters of your positions at Meet the Candidates Forums. Thank you for participating.

Sincerely,

Sample Letters

March 28, 2010

The Honorable Gregory W. Abbott
Attorney General
209 West 14th Street
Austin, TX 78701

Re: Federal Litigation: H.R. 3550—Patient Protection
and Affordable Care Act

Dear Honorable Greg Abbott:

I am a member of Friendship-West Baptist Church in Dallas, Texas, and/or a citizen in the state of Texas. I am writing to express my disappointment in your decision to join other state attorneys general and file a lawsuit with the federal government. I do not support your stated position that "no public policy goal—no matter how important or well-intentioned—can be allowed to trample the protections and rights guaranteed by our Constitution. To protect all Texans' constitutional rights, preserve the constitutional framework intended by our nation's founders, and defend our state from further infringement by the federal government, the State of Texas and other states have filed a legal challenge seeking judgment from the courts that the federal health care takeover is unconstitutional." You do not represent my voice.

It is senseless for Texas to take part in such a lawsuit. The State of Texas leads the nation in the number of uninsured adults and children. I believe the only rights being trampled on are not found in the U.S. Constitution but in the Declaration of Independence—the right to "life, liberty, and the pursuit of happiness." I support H.R. 3550 and the right to health care for all Americans. As a Texas taxpayer, I request that you cease your political posturing, dismiss the lawsuit, stop wasting my taxpayer money, and get to work on real issues, such as providing health insurance to 1.4 million Texas children, to one out of four uninsured adults in the state, and to one out of three in Dallas County who lack coverage.

"Of all the forms of inequality, injustice in healthcare is the most shocking and inhumane."

—Dr. Martin Luther King Jr.

Respectfully,

Name   Address

_____   _____

December 17, 2012

Earl Jones
Regional Vice President—Chicago Market
Clear Channel Communications

"Injustice anywhere is a threat to justice everywhere!" The words of Dr. Martin Luther King Jr. are just as true today as they were on the day he first spoke them. The injustice done to Cliff Kelley and to the black community by Clear Channel is not an injustice that will be easily overlooked or ever forgotten.

Cliff Kelley has been a responsible voice of reason and consciousness-raising in the black community for decades. Because he speaks the truth and calls the city's attention to the unjust war into which U.S. governmental policies have led us, the Clear Channel family (personal friends of the Bush administration) has chosen to "take the station in a different direction." In short, Clear Channel fired Cliff!

To add insult to injury, the voice of conscience, the voice of critical thinking, the voice of reason, and the only voice to "tell the king he has no clothes on" has been taken off the air and replaced by an entertainer and "motivational speaker." The African American community refuses to sit by idly and take this kind of insult!

We are joining with the National Coalition for Justice in Media, and we are demanding that Clear Channel put Cliff Kelley back on an FM station on Sunday mornings for two hours. You have offered Mr. Kelley (and insulted us further) a one-hour slot on an AM station that does not reach the majority of the citizens in Cook County. We refuse to accept that "mess of porridge" and sell our birthright.

We are demanding that Mr. Kelley be returned to V-103 at least by the first Sunday in February—February 5, 2006. We are demanding a new contract be signed by February 1 between Clear Channel and Cliff, or we promise you we will show you what the power of the African American community is in the city of Chicago and Cook County, Illinois.

The Clear Channel family might be used to a "finger-popping, head-bobbing, groove-enjoying black community" that does not care about social justice. If that is your "read" on the African American community in Chicago, you are sorely mistaken.

We will not tolerate this injustice, and we demand Cliff Kelley's return to an FM Clear Channel–owned station by February 1.

Sincerely,

Name (Printed)   Street Address

_____   _____

Signature   City / State / Zip

_____   _____

Name (Printed)   Street Address

_____   _____

Signature   City / State / Zip

_____   _____

July 3, 2005

Kofi A. Annan
Secretary General
United Nations
New York, NY 10017

President George W. Bush
The White House
1600 Pennsylvania Ave.
Washington, DC 20500

Dear Secretary General Annan and President Bush,

I am deeply concerned about the tragic events in the Western Darfur region of the Sudan. For over two years, Darfur has been wrought with orchestrated and planned operations of rape and murder. Estimates have suggested that over 6,000 to 10,000 people per month are being slain in this world humanitarian crisis.

Put differently, up to 400,000 people have lost their lives in Darfur since the government-sponsored genocide began in 2003. More than 2.5 million people have been displaced—their livelihoods and villages destroyed by government forces and their proxy militias—and many thousands of women and girls raped by these forces. Recent reports confirm that the government-sponsored violence continues in Darfur and that the security situation is deteriorating. The manmade humanitarian crisis in Darfur is escalating as the government of Sudan and rebel groups continue to obstruct humanitarian operations, creating famine conditions for millions of vulnerable people.

On June 23, 2004, Congress correctly called this situation genocide. The labeling of these atrocities as genocide demands now that action be taken to end the genocide. However, I continue to watch with growing anxiety and dismay as my government and the United Nations fail to respond adequately to what is described as the worst humanitarian crisis in the world.

As a concerned citizen, I write this letter strongly urging you to employ immediate action to *END THE GENOCIDE* in the Sudan.

Sincerely,

Name (Printed)   Street Address

_____   _____

Signature   City / State / Zip

_____   _____

March 30, 2003

Richard M. Daley
City Hall, Room 507
121 N. LaSalle St.
Chicago, IL 60602

Dear Mayor Daley:

    I am writing you today to urge you to make Chicago's hous-
ing crisis a top priority. The affordable housing shortage in the
city is unacceptable.
    Consider the following facts. Today in Chicago a worker
must earn $17.85 to afford a two-bedroom apartment, while
the minimum wage rests at $5.25. A family must work 139
hours per week at minimum wage ($5.25) in order to pay fair
market rent. One in five Chicago renters pays more than 50
percent of his/her income toward housing. One in five Chicago
residents lives in poverty.
    Studies show that approximately 50,000 units are needed to
meet the demand for low-income housing, and 86,000 families
are on the waiting list for Section 8 vouchers and public housing. Chicago is the only major metropolis in the country to gain
population over the past ten years while simultaneously losing
rental housing over the same period.
    Housing is considered affordable when it represents 30
percent or less of the household budget. When people pay too
much for housing, they are forced to cut corners on basic necessities, such as food, clothing, and health care. The refusal to
designate affordable housing for the residents of Chicago further
adds to the "working poor." These are persons who get up every
morning and go to work faithfully but still are not afforded the
opportunity to gain affordable housing. The refusal to designate

affordable housing for the residents of Chicago also increases the homeless population in Chicago.

With these facts in mind, a solution has been offered by Alderman Toni Preckwinckle, who has introduced a housing set-aside ordinance. This ordinance will serve to keep Chicago neighborhoods affordable.

I urge you to support housing set-asides and make affordable housing a top priority in the city of Chicago!

Sincerely,

Name (Printed)   Street Address
_____   _____

Signature   City / State / Zip
_____   _____

July 4, 2004

United States Congress

Dear Senator / Representative:

I _____, am a proud person of African ancestry. I understand that various oppressed people have been paid reparations for unfair treatment by the U.S government. Indigenous groups such as the Choctaw and Lakota people have properly received reparations for treaty violations that occurred before the emancipation of Africans in America. Japanese Americans have received reparations for their inhumane incarceration in internment camps during World War II. Jews have received reparations from other sources after the Nuremburg trials.

Chattel slavery and the triangular slave trade are recognized by international human rights organizations, e.g., the United Nations, as "crimes against humanity." As such there is no statute of limitations against nations who are to pay for these crimes.

The demand for reparations for Africans living in America and the diaspora is a demand for justice for years of injustice and inhumane treatment. This is not a request for a handout! Elected leaders and those seeking public office must recognize the truth that slavery and historical patterns of racial discrimination are the direct cause of continued increases in unemployment, substandard education, higher mortality, higher rates of incarceration, and other adverse circumstances for the descendants of Africans in America. Coupled with these inhumane facts is the engrained psychosis of racism and white supremacy among so many white Americans.

Our people have sacrificed the most for this country. In this hour in history, one seminal and major issue for black people in the upcoming election in November is the restitution for a long-standing debt of the U.S. government owed to people of African descent.

In 1898 one of the many petitions to Congress in support of a slave pension stated: "It is a precedent established by patriots of this country to relieve its distressed citizens, both on land and sea. Millions of our deceased people, besides those who still survive, worked as ex-slaves for the development of this country. . . ."

In this spirit, I sign this letter, as a descendant of those enslaved in America, in support of the just demand for reparations to the descendants of Africans who were treated unjustly and subjected to cruel and unusual punishment for nothing more than being African!

Sincerely,

Name (Printed)   Street Address
_____   _____

Signature   City / State / Zip
_____   _____

November 25, 2007

U.S. Postal Service

I write this letter in support of the Ebony Society of Philatelic Events and Reflections (ESPER) petition for a stamp honoring Dr. Samuel DeWitt Proctor.

Dr. Proctor was president of his alma mater, Virginia Union University, and later president of North Carolina A&T University. Dr. Proctor touched countless lives, including those of Dr. Martin Luther King Jr., Rev. Jesse L. Jackson Sr., and Rev. Dr. Jeremiah A. Wright Jr. Dr. Proctor also held administrative positions with the Peace Corps in Nigeria and Washington, DC, as well as the National Council of Churches. Dr. Proctor served on the governing boards of the United Negro College Fund, National Urban League, and the Overseer's Visiting Committee for the Divinity School at Harvard University. He was pastor-in-residence for the Institute for Child Advocacy at Children's Defense Fund/Haley Farm. He was awarded honorary doctoral degrees from more than fifty colleges and universities. Dr. Proctor was a prolific writer and preacher, authoring *We Have This Ministry, How Shall They Hear,* and *Sermons from the Black Pulpit,* among many others. At Rutgers University the Samuel DeWitt Proctor Chair in Education was established so that his legacy might live on.

Therefore, again, I write as a supporter of the Ebony Society of Philatelic Events and Reflections (ESPER) petition for a United States postage stamp to honor Dr. Samuel DeWitt Proctor.

Sincerely,

Name (Printed)   Street Address

_____   _____
Signature   City / State / Zip

_____   _____

April 20, 2008

Chicago Sun-Times
350 N. Orleans St. 10th Floor
Chicago, IL 60654
Agolab@suntimes.com
letters@suntimes.com

To Mr. Golab:

I write this letter to express my utter disgust for your intentional disregard of the policies and protocol of Trinity United Church of Christ made obvious by your lack of journalistic integrity.

On April 2, 2008, at a press conference called by the United Church of Christ and the National Council of Churches and hosted at Trinity United Church of Christ, members of the media were informed that Trinity was reclaiming its sacred space. At that conference, Pastor Otis Moss III stated, "If you are a member of the media looking for a church home, we welcome you. But please, leave your notepad at home and bring your Bible. We know you will experience the love of God. . . . We respect your right to report the news. Please respect our right to worship God."

On Saturday, April 12, Trinity United Church of Christ held home-going services for its longtime member and champion for justice, Judge R. Eugene Pincham. In preparation for this service, at the request of the family and to preserve the sanctity of the funeral services, press releases were distributed demanding that no media reporting be done at the funeral—especially in the sacred sanctuary during the service of worship. Moreover, as you entered the door of the church, signs were posted that read: "No video or recording devices allowed."

However, in spite of all of the aforementioned requests, even demands, to respect the sanctity of our sanctuary and church grounds and to respect the wishes of the family, you blatantly disrespected these requests. Not only did you bring your notepad into the sanctuary, but you also brought a recording device and taped the services for our member against the will of a grieving Pincham family and the judge's grieving family of faith. This is disrespectful and deplorable!

Your excuse that you did not know of the media restrictions is weak at best and is nullified by your further admission on the Cliff Kelly Show (Monday, April 14, 2008) that you would have taped even had you known of the restrictions.

This is unacceptable and immoral. We demand a public apology to Trinity United Church of Christ and to the family of Judge R. Eugene Pincham.

Sincerely,

Name (Printed)
_____

Signature
_____

Street Address
_____

City / State / Zip
_____

October 12, 2008

Honorable Richard Durbin
309 Hart SOB
Washington, DC 20510

Honorable Bobby Rush
2416 Rayburn HOB
Washington, DC 20515

Honorable Danny K. Davis
2159 Rayburn HOB
Washington, DC 20515

Honorable Barack Obama
713 Hart SOB
Washington, DC 20510

Honorable Jesse L. Jackson Jr.
2419 Rayburn HOB
Washington, DC 20515

Dear Senator/Congressman:

I write this letter to express my outrage at the congressional action of "bailing out" wealthy Wall Street at the expense of working people! Almost all economic indicators in the last several months have shown the economy is on the verge of collapse. In a much-delayed and now "celebrated" response, both Congress and Wall Street shifted the burdens of greed and decadence from the insolvent banks and mortgage companies onto the backs of the taxpayers through a multibillion-dollar bailout of those who were the cause of the dilemma. On top of a record $10.6 trillion deficit, President Bush did not blink an eye in his efforts to let corporate greed "off the hook." Home foreclosures are at a record pace as a result of unregulated predatory lending that has thousands of Americans in unyielding debt. Irresponsible and unregulated corporations will enjoy the party while the American people pay the tab.

While the current Wall Street meltdown will affect the economic health of the entire country, many African Americans will feel its tremors far more directly. When you consider that the majority of Americans live from paycheck to paycheck, any disturbance in the marketplace has an even more devastating effect on the black community when businesses are closed and jobs are eliminated. A recent study conducted by Brandeis University concluded that three out of four black middle-class families are on shaky financial ground. Black working-class families are more likely to pass on debt rather than assets to their children. There will be an even more devastating effect on the unemployed and underemployed.

This bailout represents the misplaced priorities of those who govern this country. More credence is given to profits than to the people. As we approach winter, will there be a bailout for families that cannot afford prescription medication, food, clothing, high energy bills, child care, etc.?

I ask that in the next session of Congress you sponsor legislation that:

1. Bails out families affected by the foreclosure crisis by instituting a moratorium on foreclosures until families can arrange remedial relief and restructuring mortgage loans and rates to be in line with the family income.

2. Regulate banking and finance with transparent public oversight.

3. Ban predatory lending and cap interest rates on all types of debts.

4. Provide "bail-out" relief to families adversely affected by predatory lending and job elimination.

Sincerely,

Name (Printed)   Street Address

_____   _____

Signature   City / State / Zip

_____   _____

June 21, 2009

Dear Governor Patrick Quinn/Representative Michael Madigan/
Senator John Cullerton:

I write to you as an advocate for protection from an Illinois
"Doomsday" budget that will devastate our children, our families, and our communities. It is totally unacceptable for Illinois
to function under a budget that will decimate programs for
the most vulnerable of our citizens—"my little ones," as Jesus
would frame it.

The current budget plan includes a number of proposed cuts
that would hurt children and families who already suffer from
the effects of the recession, compounding their unmet needs:

1. The proposal includes enormous reductions in funding
   for after-school programs in Illinois. Elimination of this
   funding will result in thousands of children in Illinois with
   no place to go after school. The effect will result in an increase in at-risk youth, which always has a negative effect
   on our communities. Additionally, these cuts may cause a
   loss of jobs to after-school providers if programs need to
   shut down, a reduction in services provided to children, or
   increased parent fees for programming.

2. Last year Illinois became the first state in the country to
   provide state funding for homeless education programs.
   The State Board of Education just awarded grants under
   this program in February 2009 to school districts statewide. These school districts have committed to launching
   new strategies to ensure success in school for homeless
   children. Those programs will have to end after three
   months if the state eliminates this program.

3. DCFS finalizing decisions in how to manage cuts totaling
   close to $500 million will result in higher worker-to-foster-
   child caseload ratios, a 50 percent reduction in care reim-
   bursements for foster parents, and close to a 20 percent in
   foster children residential rates.

4. Programs such as Healthy Families Illinois, Parents Too Soon, and Illinois Children's Mental Health Partnership, and social services agencies such as Centers for New Horizons, will face elimination or drastic reduction in services and staffing.

5. Up to 80,000 families—roughly 150,000 children—will lose their child care. Illinois's next state budget should reflect a lesson that every parent knows from experience and that research confirms: young children's learning experiences today build a vital foundation for their success tomorrow.

In addition to the cuts above, this "Doomsday" budget will not only affect our children but the citizens in Illinois who need the most help. If this budget passes, cuts will affect those in need of substance abuse intervention and mental health assistance, health care for the most vulnerable of society, senior care and support, sexual assault victim support, and state scholarships for those trying to better themselves through education.

A massive state deficit and a poor national economy certainly present challenges. Yet it is critical that Illinois protect the network of early childhood policies and programs we have assembled to strengthen the healthy development of children from birth to age five. We cannot afford to risk our children's lives. We urge you to pass a budget that ensures a healthy and safe environment for our young people and the most vulnerable of our society so they can become productive and responsible citizens in our lives. Not to do so will cost the state much more than you are trying to preserve at this point. Their future, and our future as a state, will depend on the stance you take at this moment.

Sincerely,

Name (Printed)   Street Address
_____   _____

Signature   City / State / Zip
_____   _____

March 21, 2012

President Barack Obama
The White House
1600 Pennsylvania Ave.
Washington, DC 20500

Dear President Obama,

I am deeply concerned about the tragic events in the metropolitan Chicago area. During the weekend of March 16–18
alone, more than 49 people have been shot and 10 people killed
from gun violence. If that's not enough, statistics from the
Chicago Police Department detail that shootings have increased
by 27 percent and homicides have increased by 32 percent this
year over last year! This is in no uncertain terms a humanitarian
crisis that demands the attention of not only the communities
but the government!

As the murders attributed to gun violence continue to esca-
late, so does the grief of families. What is even more disheart-
ening is to understand that had many of these killings taken
place in areas other than African American communities, there
probably would have been a public outcry to stop the violence.
In this current election season, it appears that the culture of
violence affecting youth is not even on the agenda of those vying
for our vote. We see this clearly in the case of Trayvon Martin,
the rising murder rate in metropolitan Chicago area, and other
urban centers across the country.

Desperate times call for desperate measures. We are reaching
out to you, Mr. President, to reach out and provide some assistance in quelling the tide of violence. We are not asking for more
police on the streets. We are asking for some substantive action

that would get guns off the street and provide more resources for violence prevention.

As people simply watch while people are continuously killed, we are witnessing nothing less than genocide. The labeling of these atrocities as genocide demands now that action be taken to end the genocide.

As a concerned citizen, I write this letter strongly urging you to employ immediate action to end the genocide on the killing fields of Chicago.

Sincerely,

Name (Printed)
_____

Signature
_____

Street Address
_____

City / State / Zip
_____

DATE

Richard Land
Southern Baptist Convention
SBC Ethics & Religious Liberty Commission
901 Commerce Street, #600
Nashville, TN 37203

Dear Reverend Land:

I write to express my sincere disgust and strong discontent over the comments uttered by you in such poor taste regarding the response of African American Leaders to the murder of Trayvon Martin.

As you well know, the Southern Baptist Convention was founded because said founders did not want to give up their enslaved Africans in 1845. The founders of the Convention saw the enslaved Africans as property and not people. Based on such a perspective, their lives were expendable. It is clear from your comments that you see African American people through the same lenses as the founders of the Southern Baptist Convention. In no uncertain terms, your racist rant that "a black man is statistically more likely to do you harm than a white man" shows just how out of touch you are with reality. What statistics support your argument, or is it just your own privileged perspective? Further, for you to criticize President Obama, Reverend Jackson, and Reverend Sharpton for standing up and speaking out on behalf of the family of Trayvon Martin also reveals the white supremacist privileged perspective from which you come. It is because of comments like yours and racist perspectives that persist in our convention and in this country that a culture of violence against African American life exists in this country. When leaders such as yourself issue such vitriolic and demonic expressions, a culture of hate is further perpetrated. Moreover, such comments expose the entrenched racist perspectives that still permeate the Southern Baptist Convention.

As a concerned citizen and person of faith, I wholeheartedly deplore your comments. I am aware that you have issued an apology, and such apology is accepted under great suspicion. I truly believe that had you gotten no press coverage on your statements, you would not have apologized, for you yourself clearly stated that you have no regrets regarding your remarks.

Finally, you should know that as long as black children are being killed in cold blood with minimal accountability, as long as the laws of this country continue to favor the white wealthy and privileged, as long as resources for African American children and families are being shortchanged, as along as the length of life and how well one learns are determined by one's zip code, as long as the prison industrial complex continues to target men and women and boys and girls of African descent, and as long as racism rears its ugly head in the parish or politics, domestically or in this denomination, you can be sure that I will speak out against injustice! For in the words of our Lord and Savior, "The Spirit of the Lord is upon me, because he has anointed me to bring good news to the poor. He has sent me to proclaim release to the captives and recovery of sight to the blind, to let the oppressed go free, to proclaim the year of the Lord's favor" (Luke 4:18-19 NRSV)

Sincerely,

Name   Street Address
_____   _____

Signature   City / State / Zip
_____   _____

Additional Resources

Hendricks, Jr. Obery M. *The Politics of Jesus: Rediscovering the True Revolutionary Nature of Jesus' Teachings and How They Have Been Corrupted.* New York: Three Leaves, 2007. http://isbndb.com/d/publisher/three_leaves_press.html.

In this book, Dr. Obery Hendricks examines how the teachings of Jesus have either been taken out of context, co-opted, or simply watered down. Hendricks examines how the historical and cultural roots of the people from whom Jesus came informed his theological stance. Further, Hendricks posits seven strategies that Jesus employed in his efforts to bring his prophetic justice-seeking ministry to bear on the politics of his day so that the Kingdom of God would be established on earth as it is in Heaven.

Jacobsen, Dennis A. *Doing Justice: Congregations and Community Organizing.* Minneapolis: Fortress, 2001. http://fortresspress.com/.

This excellent resource outlines key principles for organizing congregations and communities around issues of justice. Jacobsen employs many of the training tips taught by the Gamaliel Foundation and provides practical tools for efforts to organize for justice.

Tune, Romal. *VOTE Training Manual.* Clergy Strategic Alliances, LLC, 1380 Monroe St. NW, #1111, Washington, DC, 20010. http://www.csastrategies.com/programs/vote-engagement/.

The *VOTE Training Manual* contains organizing tips for "getting out the Vote." It is an excellent resource that should be used by any church concerned about educating and inspiring congregants and communities about the implementation and power of the vote.

Whelchel, L.H. *The History and Heritage of African-American Churches: A Way Out of No Way.* St. Paul, MN: Paragon House, 2011.

The History and Heritage of African American Churches is a rich resource which shows the roots of the African American Church beginning anthropologically with the African origins of humanity. Whelchel masterfully connects the dots from those African origins through the sick and sadistic system of chattel slavery, particularly detailing how the Black church not only came to be, but also came to change the world through various struggles and movements. This book should also be read in conversation with the classic text by Dr. Gayraud Wilmore entitled *Black Religion and Black Radicalism: An Interpretation of the Religious History of African Americans* (Maryknoll, NY; Orbis Books, 1998 3rd ed.). In this text, Wilmore documents the religious history of African Americans and its contribution to the cause of liberation for African people.